GERARD MANLEY HOPKINS

Sean Sheehan

GREENWICH EXCHANGE
LONDON

Greenwich Exchange, London

First published in Great Britain in 2005
All rights reserved
Revised edition 2006

Gerard Manley Hopkins
© Sean Sheehan 2005

Printed and bound by Q3 Digital/Litho, Loughborough
Tel: 01509 213456
Typesetting and layout by Albion Associates, London
Tel: 020 8852 4646
Cover design by December Publications, Belfast
Tel: 028 90286559

Cover: Gerard Manley Hopkins © Getty Images/Hulton Archive

Greenwich Exchange Website: www.greenex.co.uk

ISBN 1-871551-77-3

Contents

Chronology   v

1   Being Hopkins   1

2   Poems of Inscape and Instress   22

3   A Stranger in a Strange Land   39

4   Hopkins and the Critics   52

Conclusion   62

Further Reading   66

Chronology

1844   Born at Stratford, London, on 2nd July.

1852   His family moves to Oak Hill, Hampstead, and he attends a local day school.

1854   Becomes a boarder at Highgate School, near Hampstead, and excels academically.

1860   Tours southern Germany with his father.

1863-67   Wins a Classical Exhibition to Balliol College, Oxford, and meets Robert Bridges at university. Keeps Diaries, until 1866, and records descriptions and sketches of nature, word lists and drafts of early poems.

1866-75   Starts a private Journal, develops a theory of 'inscape' and 'instress'.

1866   Decides to leave the Church of England and become a Roman Catholic.

1867-78   Graduates with a First, and begins teaching in a Catholic school in Birmingham.

1868   Decides to become a Jesuit priest and burns his early poems.

1870-73   Studies philosophy as part of his Jesuit training.

1874-77 Studies theology at St Bueno's College in north Wales.

1875-76 Writes 'The Wreck of the Deutschland'.

1877 Ordained as a Jesuit priest.

1878-79 Works as a priest in London for a short period, then at Church of St Aloysius in Oxford where he is also the chaplain to Cowley Barracks.

1880-81 Works as a priest at St Francis Xavier's in Liverpool. Works also for a short period as the parish priest at St Joseph's church in Glasgow.

1882-4 Teaches classics at Stoneyhurst College.

1884-9 Appointed Professor of Greek and Latin at University College, Dublin.

1889 Dies in Dublin of typhoid fever on 8th June and is buried in Glasnevin Cemetery, Dublin.

1893 Bridges publishes 11 of Hopkins' poems in *Poets and Poetry of the Century*.

1915 Bridges publishes six of his poems in *The Spirit of Man*.

1918 Bridges edits the published *Poems of Gerard Manley Hopkins*.

1

Being Hopkins

There is something rather pleasing about the puzzling nature of Gerard Manley Hopkins. On the one hand there is the ascetic, ultra-pious young man who embraces a 19th-century form of religious fundamentalism by deciding at the age of 23 to become a Jesuit. He approvingly submits to the authoritarian and highly disciplined order of the Jesuits and allows the narrative of the rest of his life to be dictated by them. Moved from pillar to post, sometimes with less than a day's notice, Hopkins is shuffled from Jesuit colleges to various churches in London, Oxford, Manchester, Liverpool and Glasgow. Then in 1884, at the age of 39, he is shipped off to Dublin to teach Greek and mark examination papers at the fledgling Catholic university of Dublin. He would probably have been moved again if the combined effect of pressure of work, mental exhaustion and a bout of typhoid had not killed him five years later. His passing went unremarked by most of those who knew him; as a shy, self-effacing man who was hard to get to know and with few friends, this is hardly surprising. Hopkins was unknown as a poet and although he had occasionally bumped into W.B. Yeats in Dublin, Yeats never remembered the meetings. By the time James Joyce arrived at University College, Dublin as a student, nine years later, Hopkins had been forgotten.

Yet this deeply submissive, outwardly conventional and re-actionary Victorian not only writes some of the most exciting English poetry of the 19th century but does so by developing a poetic form that is revolutionary for its time. Celebrating the natural world, feeling melancholy at the passing of time and the poignancy of life, these are very conventional subjects for poetry and especially so in the English poetical tradition of the 19th century, but Hopkins makes these his subjects in a language that is radically different to the prevailing orthodoxies. Hopkins was revolutionary because of the way he wrote, not because of what he wrote about. Rejecting traditional notions of poetic verisimilitude as an aesthetic response to the world, Hopkins seems to pre-empt modernism by bringing to the foreground the very medium of his art. This medium, language, is no longer seen as a means for transferring a thought or a sense impression. Language becomes the subject, as it did for Joyce and other modernist writers and, like Joyce, Hopkins found he could not express himself within the existing literary modes. He was trying, he said, "to express a subtle and recondite thought on a subtle and recondite subject in a subtle and recondite way".

During his lifetime, when there was no one to appreciate his artistic endeavour, Hopkins never lost faith in his own way of writing poetry and persisted along his chosen path. Condemned to become a very private poet, there are only his writings – prose and poetry – to remind us of his valorous individuality, his integrity and independence of mind and his personal, passionate engagement with life. In more ways than one, Hopkins felt alienated from his society and this estrangement helped him see the social reality of his world from the perspective of the Other:

> ... in a manner I am a Communist ... it is a dreadful thing for the greatest and most necessary part of a very rich nation to live a hard life without dignity, knowledge, comforts, delight, or hopes in the midst of plenty – which plenty they make. They profess that they do not care what they wreck and burn, the old civilisation and order must be destroyed. This is a dreadful look out but what has the old civilisation done for them? As it as present stands in England it is itself in great measure founded upon wrecking. But they got none of the spoils, they came in for nothing but harm from it then and

thereafter ... The more I look the more black and deservedly black the future looks, so I will write no more.

Hopkins rarely shared such an outlook with his acquaintances – knowing so few who would listen or respond – and like so much of his self he kept it submerged. Such an outlook coexisted, though not as uneasily as we might think it would, with quite reactionary expressions of political and social thought on Hopkins' part. This helps explain why, when it is divorced from an understanding of Hopkins' philosophy, his letter on communism comes as a surprise and a shock. Notwithstanding this, his poetry often has a similar kind of effect. There is a sharpness of outlook, an ecstatic celebration of natural beauty, an awareness of sorrow, experience of despair and a verbal adventurousness that, for most readers coming to his verse for the first time, strikes one as astonishingly vivid and memorable. There is a frisson of delight upon first being introduced to Hopkins' poems and they remain refreshingly personal and honest – and trying to understand what it is about his poetry that can so arrest a reader's attention brings one to the heart of his achievement.

Hopkins sees delight all around him in nature and for secular readers imbues moments of natural, transitory beauty with a pagan-like sensuality, while also bringing to such moments a metaphysical magic. What becomes clear is Hopkins' especial fascination with the nature of language and the relationship between language and reality. More so than any other aspect, it is Hopkins' insistent concern with the nature of language that helps make his poetry sound so modern and so un-Victorian. Although all poets are especially concerned with language and its relationship with reality, what makes Hopkins seem like a modernist artist is his very self-conscious engagement with the medium of his art and his deliberate, innovative exploration of the form of poetry. At a philosophical level, Hopkins wanted to understand and relate language to the world of existence; a world that existed apparently independent of language and yet in some way was bound up with it.

A way of coming at Hopkins' poetry and appreciating his achievement, albeit in a sideways manner, is by relating his fascination with language to the concerns of some thinkers in Germany and England who changed the face of philosophy in the decades after the poet's death. At the time that Robert Bridges was intent on keeping most of Hopkins' poetry unpublished, in the belief that the public would not be able to handle it, two important European philosophers – Bertrand Russell and Gottlob Frege – were finding it impossible to put aside questions about language and reality. They were determined to sort out some basic issues that were bedevilling philosophy and, as Hopkins had been, they were strongly opposed to the philosophical fashion of the times that saw the mind, consciousness, as the creator and shaper of meaning. Countering this intellectual fashion, they wanted to insist that language referred directly to the real world outside of the self, and in a way that was not dependent upon, or shaped by, an intellectual component supplied by the mind. This search for a secure, logical, basis for making valid statements about the world led them into some fairly esoteric corners but their intention, like Hopkins', was the humble one of insisting on truth as something that could be kept free of psychological contamination.

The philosopher Wittgenstein was born in 1889, the year that Hopkins died, and, in the same year that Bridges finally brought out an edition of Hopkins' poetry, 1918, Wittgenstein was completing a venerable and highly modernist account of the relationship between language, thought and reality. It would bring together and crystallize a way of looking at language with a startling degree of sophistication. The fundamental role of language, claimed Wittgenstein, was to name and describe bits of reality. Every name has a meaning and the meaning is to be found in the object for which it stands. Every sentence describes a state of affairs that is made up of objects, hence the names in a sentence. Second, a relationship that might happen to exist between those objects is mirrored in the grammar of a sentence. The logical syntax of a sentence projects, or mirrors, a bit of reality because the relationship between a set of objects is capable of being reflected in the relationship that the grammar enacts. Language is linked with reality because the possible relationships between objects that are expressed in a sentence are the same possible relationships that could logically exist in the world.

The purpose of mentioning Russell, Frege and the early Wittgenstein, is to emphasise the profoundly philosophical nature of what Hopkins was concerned with in his exploration of how language and reality might inter-connect. Both Hopkins and the early Wittgenstein, writing in different disciplines and bringing different philosophical nuances to their work, are both possessed with the idea that language is indissolubly bound up with the way things are, the world out there. The ontology of Hopkins' poetry, like the philosophy of the early Wittgenstein, is realist. What is meant by realism here is the belief, serving as a foundation, in a real, solid world existing out there beyond human consciousness. Hopkins and Wittgenstein, who despite their many differences have interesting similarities in terms of character, both share the conviction that language is capable of reaching right up to reality. Hopkins' poetry is not a philosophical text but the philosophical idea fuelling his poetry is this conviction.

Ironically, Bridges' rationale for censoring Hopkins' poetry for nearly thirty years after the poet's death arose from his certainty that Hopkins' use of language was eccentric and the cause of problems for readers. He writes in the introduction to the first edition in 1918 about Hopkins' breach of "literary decorum" – as if writing good poetry is like the kind of social occasion where some people feel obliged to choose a particular form of dress – and how he "neglects the need that there is for care in the placing of words that are grammatically ambiguous ... and he will sometimes so arrange such words that a reader looking for a verb may find that he has two or three ambiguous monosyllables from which to select".

What for Bridges was a deficiency that needed to be apologised for is likely to be an essential aspect of what most readers today find attractive and energising about Hopkins' verse. It helps to always bear in mind Hopkins' own advice – "take breath and read it with the ears, as I always wish to be read, and my verse becomes all right":

> How to kéep – is there ány any, is there none such, nowhere
> known some, bow or brooch or braid or brace, láce,
> latch or catch or key to keep
> Back beauty, keep it, beauty, beauty, beauty, ... from vanishing
> away?

When these lines from 'The Leaden Echo and the Golden Echo' are read aloud, the urgency of the poet communicates itself in the verve of the constantly changing alliteration and the progression of the assonance. Hopkins' voice is heard in the insistent questioning, in the dramatic stopping power and the semantic implication of "Back" (this word, explained Hopkins, "is not pretty, but it gives that feeling of physical constraint which I want"). The last two lines of the verse here, with the fading effect of the repetition and the conclusion to the rhetorical question, aurally register the melancholy timbre of the passage as a whole.

This can only be the starting point for any appreciation of Hopkins and we are not going to be satisfied with merely emoting over the transitoriness of beauty, however mellifluously expressed. It is because Hopkins himself could not be satisfied in this way that he found it impossible to write poetry like his fellow Victorians, impelled instead to develop his own poetics to explain and justify his concerns. Hopkins' notions of inscape, instress and sprung rhythm, which we will shortly come to, arise from his conviction that language can touch reality. Language, lying alongside reality in the way that a ruler comes up against and lies alongside what is being measured, bears an ontological force because of this. Often, impatiently, Hopkins wants us to just use our senses so that we can see the truth of what his poetry is enacting. The opening two lines of 'The Starlight Night' ("Look at the stars! look, look up at the skies!/ O look at all the fire-folk sitting in the air!"), with their thrice-repeated "look", their imperatives and imperative punctuation, state in simple words what was a simple truth for the poet, and they help us understand what Hopkins meant when he said that what you look hard at seems to look hard at you. Not surprisingly perhaps, 'The Starlight Night' has been found wanting, open as it is to the charge of being wistful and whimsical but this fault-finding, like the criticism of 'Spring' for being a conservative, escapist-like idyll, ignores the metaphysical weight that Hopkins brings to the relationship between being and language.

The medieval Duns Scotus (1266-1308), Hopkins' favourite philosopher, provided him with theological support for his metaphysics. Although not officially endorsed by the Jesuits, Scotus' idea that every object's being, its 'this-ness' (*haecceitas*), was a unique quality that revealed its fundamental divinity, served to help justify what Hopkins was drawing attention to in his poetry. For Scotus, it was existence and not some Platonic essence that mattered and this could be experienced intuitively, not rationally. Hopkins' use of italics in the impassioned 'As kingfishers catch fire, dragonflies draw flame' explicitly asserts this to be the case:

> Each mortal thing does one thing and the same:
>   Deals out that being indoors each one dwells;
> Selves – goes itself; *myself* it speaks and spells,
> Crying *What I do is me: for that I came.*

The selfness of a being, that being which dwells "indoors" in each single thing, is what gives it identity. For all being, selfness is inseparable from doing; it is in doing that the self is posited ("*myself* it speaks") and makes itself known.

'Being' as a philosophical term – it may help to think of its meaning in terms of 'existence' or 'actuality', as something dynamic and tangible, not passive – and the importance that Hopkins brought to the term shows how keen was his independence of thought. The acceptable philosophy of Hopkins' age featured a subject, the human mind or consciousness, and an object, the external world. The relationship between the two, between subject and object, "us and things" as Hopkins put it, and the extent to which the mind filtered or shaped our perception of the world, was the stuff of Victorian intellectual debate. Hopkins rejected the metaphysical implications of the dominant philosophical model of his time (and our times too): the Kantian model of a subject – you, I or anyone – receiving disparate impressions of an object, the world, which is in a permanent state of flux and permanently unknowable as to its essential nature. Hopkins adopted an alternative metaphysic that came from his reading of the ancient Greek philosopher, Parmenides, and from his introduction to the thought of Hegel through T.H. Green, one of his tutors at university.

The Pre-Socratic Parmenides expounded his philosophy in the first half of the 5th century BCE in a poem of which little more than a hundred lines survive. It is the earliest known piece of philosophical argument in Western philosophy and, for the first time in the West, wonder is expressed at the sheer being of existence. Reading and thinking about Parmenides at university, Hopkins makes his own notes and early in 1868, for the first time, he introduces two terms of his own – "instress" and "inscape" – that become a key to understanding his own poetics. "His great text," writes Hopkins referring to the surviving fragments of Parmenides "means that all things are upheld by instress and are meaningless without it". Instress becomes Hopkins' term for the energy, or stress, that makes being meaningful; without instress reality would be only a meaningless flux. Hopkins also first mentions inscape when writing of Parmenides and how "[h]is feeling for instress, for the flush and foredrawn, and for inscape is most striking". Inscape is clearly related to instress and the nature of the distinction between the two terms emerges later in Hopkins' writings. Inscape becomes his term for the pattern which manifests the inner selfhood of a thing, that which is referred to in the lines from 'As kingfishers catch fire, dragonflies draw flame' as "that being indoors ... *myself* it speaks". When the inscape of something makes itself known to someone it exerts its instress. When Hopkins writes in his journal about the different ways in which the world excites him, he often does so in terms of instress and inscape – sometimes as nouns, other times as verbs – and in ways that suggest that one need not labour over trying to keep the two terms too separate and distinct. When, for example, Hopkins admires a Giotto painting in the National Gallery he writes of "the instress of loveliness" in the artist's work; another time he writes how "[u]nless you refresh the mind from time to time you cannot always remember or believe how deep the inscape of things is".

Being just *is* – something that Hopkins noted when translating Parmenides for himself. "[it] lies by itself, the selfsame thing abiding in the selfsame place: so it abides, steadfast there" – and agreeing with Parmenides that the only coherent thing that can be said of anything is that it *is*: "sweet earth ... canst but be", as he says in 'Ribblesdale':

> But indeed I have often felt when I have been in this mood and felt the depth of an instress or how fast the inscape holds a thing that nothing is so pregnant and straightforward to the truth as simple *yes* and *is*.

Being's primacy – the wonder of there being something rather than nothing – was emphasized by Parmenides and Hopkins responded to the Greek philosopher's insistence that things are, they exist. Being includes language and as a result language possesses an authenticity because it is capable of manifesting the wonder of existence. The ontological force behind the verb

9

'to be' that allows us to say 'this exists' or 'that is red' is a fundamental idea that Hopkins expresses in his notes. Being takes in language: it is alive and, like the grandeur of God, it is 'charged'. Being is truth, inaugural, whole, unchangeable ("past change" in 'Pied Beauty'), not subject to the whims or the mental structures of the human subject. Being without this sense would mean that language could only record a succession of sense impressions from the meaningless flux of reality and language would break down if never able to get beyond an ever-vanishing, fugitive reality. Being in language provides the "stem" or "stress" which carries the mind over into things and, reciprocally, things into the mind. This is the idea that enables Hopkins to reject, or transcend, the subject-object division that Kant had enshrined in philosophical thought. In Kantian thought, the mind of the subject makes acquaintance with the objects of the external world but is never able to go beyond the phenomena and see what is really there. What can be known arises from the external world but is filtered by structures in the subjective consciousness of the human subject. Hopkins was introduced to a radically different philosophy by the Hegelian, T.H. Green, one that dissolves the dualism of subject and objects and allowed for a sense of being that is shared by both subject and object. The being of consciousness is described by Hopkins as a "bridge" that collapses the Kantian distinction between appearance and the deeper reality behind appearance. This idea is expressed in 'Hurrahing in Harvest':

And the azurous hung hills are his world-wielding shoulder
Majestic – as a stallion stalwart, very-violet-sweet! –
These things, these things were here and but the beholder
Wanting; which two when they once meet,
The heart rears wings bold and bolder
And hurls for him, O half hurls earth for him off under his
    feet.

Words are also capable of possessing inscape because of their ability to reach down to the instress that makes being meaningful.

In poetry, for Hopkins, the inscape and instress of being coexist with the inscape that words are capable of possessing and displaying. This is what he meant by saying, "poetry is in fact only employed to carry the inscape of speech for the inscape's sake". Poetry, he went on to explain, is "speech framed to be heard for its own sake and interest even over and above its interest or meaning".

In that most famous of his poems, 'The Windhover', Hopkins responds to the sight of a kestrel in flight – a suitably conventional occasion for a poetic celebration of nature's wonder – but the bird's wild beauty is not recorded as merely the result of a sensitive, but nonetheless subjective, reaction on the part of an observer-poet. The uniqueness of the moment recorded in the poem is not reducible to something predictably symbolic – of God, of Beauty or whatever – because essentially it is an ontological moment. What is implied by saying the moment is ontological (from an ancient Greek word meaning *being*) is that what matters is that the bird, displaying attributes 'caught' by the poet, exists in that moment of time and in that particular place. The poet is not simply investing or imbuing the moment with meaning, either of the mystical, the magical or religious variety, because the meaning *is* the bird's existence and the bird's existence at that moment is its meaning. This is not a matter of symbolism but of ontology.

The poem does recreate the experience of seeing the bird, and it is an important experience for the poet-observer, but at a more fundamental level the poem's language is recreating the kestrel's being at that moment. It is part of what Hopkins meant when he said that his poetry must be read aloud: "till it is spoken it is not performed, it does not perform, it is not itself". What is *not* meant here is the familiar notion that a poem brings alive and recreates a subjective moment of experience. It is the sheer being of the bird, its 'this-ness' that makes itself known to the poet. In realising this, the poet also realises how such moments of awareness and knowledge of the world can escape our attention: his own heart was "in hiding" just before catching sight of the kestrel. Awareness of existence in this way, of our own self and that of other phenomena, is part of that "delight" that Hopkins in his letter (see p.2 above) sees as being denied to the dispossessed of his society. The citizens (denizens) who are rendered unemployed in 'Tom's Garland' are "[U]ndenizened, beyond bound/Of earth's glory, earth's ease": Hopkins sees the connections between political power, social exclusion, moral self-worth and ownership of the environment, remarking to his mother in a letter that everyone, regardless of their wealth, is "owner of the skies and stars and everything wild that is to be found on the earth".

Metaphysics and poetry come together because it is possible for words to literally bear witness to the instress of the world and celebrate the beauty of inscape. Hopkins writes of a particular mode of thought that "catches" the wonder of being; the verb here expressing the epistemological breakthrough that poetry is capable of achieving. The conventional thinking of Hopkins' age was that poetry was about 'feeling' not cognition. Epistemology, the study of what can be known, was the province of science, not poetry. Hopkins rejects the binary-like opposition of these two ideas. He has no truck with what can be labelled the Matthew Arnold school of poetry, the notion that genuine poetry comes from the soul, that we emote in response to the poet's sensibilities, and that the cultured appreciation of classic literary masterpieces provides us with a set of touchstones to assay the worth of a poetic enterprise. His friend Robert Bridges, following this pedagogy, did try to encourage him to read classic literary works in the hope that they would make Hopkins' own style less eccentric. It would be to no avail: the studying of masterpieces, said Hopkins, only made him "admire, and do otherwise". Far from setting poetry and science up in opposition to one another, Hopkins followed with interest the new developments of his age in the field of physics and saw what scientists were revealing as further examples of his own metaphysics. As Gillian Beer (see Further Reading) has shown, some of the less-easily comprehensible lines in 'The Blessed Virgin compared to the Air we Breathe' are dependent on an understanding of what Tyndall established in 1870, that particles in the atmosphere refract the sun's rays and, depending on the wavelength, register with us as colour. Hopkins happily absorbed what Tyndall and the field of spectroscopy had to offer, as he did the whole new field of energy physics. The new ontology of this physics finds its way into celebratory poems like 'As kingfishers catch fire, dragonflies draw flame' and 'That Nature is a Heraclitean Fire and of the comfort of the Resurrection', and the memorable opening lines of 'God's Grandeur' with an image that is electrifying in more ways than one:

> The world is charged with the grandeur of God.
> It will flame out, like shining from shook foil;

Hopkins seeks a poetic form that will recognise being, what he calls stress, and its bridging of the gulf between the self and the world. In his journal he wrote of how "there are ten thousand men and ten thousand things for them to think of but they are but names given and taken, eye and lip service to the truth, husks and inscapes of it: the truth itself, the burl [of Being]". An 'instress' is a moment, an instance, of such being – the prefix 'in' denoting its internal unity – and 'inscape' is its specificity. Words, especially in poetry, arise from and acknowledge being, but our existence is also part of being and we are at one with the world in this respect. There is a structure of relationships between us and the world, built upon a system of differences. Hopkins' early partiality for an onomatopoeic account of language was part of his desire for a language that could reach down to individual being, a poetic voice that could constitute and enshrine the presence of being. This was the poetry of inscape, a heightened and disciplined form of living speech and one with a deep grammar that could survive a personal style that might otherwise seem idiosyncratic. The style – incomplete

13

sentences, missing pronouns and conjunctions, ellipsis of expression, neologisms, embedded propositions – was felt to be necessary by Hopkins in order to be able to enact the distinctiveness of inscaped speech. Without inscape, understanding and knowledge was in danger of relying on pure intuition and the punctual, fleetingly insignificant present.

Hopkins' fascination with using language to capture the 'this-ness' of a natural phenomenon is evident in his prose writings from a young age, and years later he would extract details from his youthful diary in the composition of poems. A few weeks before his 23rd birthday, Hopkins writes: "Carnations if you look close have their tongue-shaped petals powdered with spankled [sparkling] red glister, which no doubt gives them their brilliancy: sharp, chip shadows of one petal on another; the notched edge curls up and so is darked, which gives them graceful precision." He seeks to impersonally record what it is about a phenomenon that gives it a special identity – observing young lambs frolicking in a field, he thinks "it is as if it were the earth that flung them, not themselves" – and when he does involve his personal self it is often because he wants to emphasise the autonomy of his subject matter. Aged around thirty, but still before bringing himself to resume the writing of poetry, he records the quality of a summer evening's gentle wind using images that rule out any idea of the individual affecting the scene; the evening's moment takes hold of him and he merely inhabits it temporarily:

> Very hot, though the wind, which was south, dappled very sweetly on one's face and when I came out I seemed to put it on like a gown as a man puts on the shadow he walks into and hoods or hats himself with the shelter of a roof, a penthouse, or a copse of trees, I mean it rippled and fluttered like light linen, one could feel the folds and braids of it ...

Hopkins' own term, inscape, is closely linked to the idea that the essential 'this-ness' of objects in the world can be experienced in a deeper way than our everyday, un-empathetic awareness tends to permit. The 'scape' is phenomena that we experience in an un-empathetic mode while the prefix 'in' suggests the intrinsic, essential form that gives something its being. This is brought out in a remark Hopkins made of a painting, "Intense expression of face, expression of character, not mood, true inscape." Mood is an expression of personality but character, we want to say, goes deeper into the being of an individual. Instress is an act of emotional cognition and it is related to inscape in that, in the act of instress, the being of something is apprehended in a charged moment.

"Sprung rhythm" is Hopkins' term for his way of communicating his inscapes in poetry. Technically, it is his system of metre based on regulating the number of stresses in a line, in place of the more established system of counting the number of syllables in a line. Some accounts of Hopkins' sprung rhythm can make it sound esoteric or just odd but it is not difficult to understand and appreciate, especially when sustained in a long poem. In 'The Wreck of the Deutschland', the stresses follow a 2-3-4-3-5-5-4-6 pattern (in Part 2 the first line has three stresses) –

> I díd say yés
> O at líghtning and láshed ród;
> Thou héardst me trúer than tóngue conféss
> Thy térror, O Chríst, O Gód;
> Thou knówest the wálls, áltar and hoúr and níght:
> The swóon of a héart that the swéep and the húrl of thee tród
> Hárd dówn with a hórror of héight:
> And the mídriff astráin with léaning of, láced with fíre of stréss.

– and are intimately related to the meaning of any particular stanza. In the second stanza above, for instance, the scanning brings home (they "fetch out" as Hopkins put it) the severity and duration of his trial. In 'Spelt from Sibyl's Leaves', where Hopkins strives to bring out the chant-like timing of the poem, he unusually adopts an eight-stress line.

Hopkins' conscious motive in developing a theory of sprung rhythm was to imitate the natural rhythm of spoken English, "the least forced, the most rhetorical and emphatic of all possible rhythms", and yet keep it co-existing with the rigours of poetic form. Hopkins explained what he was striving to do in a letter to his brother:

> Sprung rhythm gives back to poetry its true soul and self. As poetry is emphatically speech purged of dross like gold in the furnace, so it must have emphatically the essential elements of speech. Now emphasis itself, stress, is one of these: sprung rhythm makes verse stressy.

Hopkins recognises the fact that poetry is closer to speech and this recognition helps account for many of the features of his style that Bridges thought were idiosyncratic. Far from being eccentric, Hopkins was setting out to compose verse without the artificiality that characterises prose. From this point of view it is prose, with its strict linear progression from one sentence to the next, that is idiosyncratic. When people talk naturally to one another they tend not to speak in sentences – it is an oddity characteristic of a peculiar kind of middle-class person to think that they always speak in sentences and endeavour to do so – but instead – frequently omitting the linking words that the grammar of written English requires, fluently embedding propositions and being elliptical all at the same time – use pitch and tone of voice, vary the pace and volume and employ repetitions, hesitations and facial expressions to express meaning. How we feel about what we are saying and to whom we are speaking registers itself in shifting patterns of speech, bodily movement and the body's breathing. Hopkins is interested in the rhythms of spoken English because he is seeking to restore to verse the emotional charge that ordinary speech can exhibit when thought and language are fused expressively and without overdue concern for conventional niceties of syntax and grammar. Hopkins' theory conceives of language as originally mimesis, an imitation in the mind and mouth of distinctive facets of being. Language possesses the world, not in the sense of rudely taking and having but by way of mimetic appropriation, a dynamic imitation of the world. This is what Hopkins was getting at when he wrote to Coventry Patmore on 24th October 1887:

> When I read your prose and Newman's and some modern writers' the same impression is borne in on me; no matter how beautiful the thought, nor, taken singly, with what happiness expressed you do not know what *writing prose* is. At bottom what you do is to think aloud, to think with pen and paper. In this process there are advantages; they may outweigh those of a perfect technic; but they exclude the belonging technic, the belonging rhetoric, the own proper eloquence of written prose. Each thought is told off singly and there follows a pause and this breaks the continuing, the strain of address which writing shared usually have. The beauty, the eloquence, of good prose cannot come wholly from the thought.

The heart of Hopkins' whole philosophy of life was that to make the most of being alive meant being responsive and respectful to the being of the world. This lies at the root of his alienation and his estrangement from Victorian civilisation and it helps explain why he could think of himself as a kind of communist. The "wrecking" that he says is characteristic of his age is born of the capitalists' drive to exploit earth's natural resources and other people at the expense of the instress and the individuality of being that they ignore in the pure pursuit of profit. Hopkins expresses this in the sestet of 'God's Grandeur':

> ... all is seared with trade; bleared, smeared with toil;
> And wears man's smudge and shares man's smell: ...

The poem contrasts the wonderful freshness of the world with the filthy, narcissistic impulse of mercantile mankind. In notes written in 1868 he castigates what he calls the "positivists" of his age, "those are quite grimed with the concrete", a class that only sees the world in terms of exploitable appearances. What is ultimately polluted is respect for the fullness of Being and the beauty of existence and the poet's disgust is expressed in terms of a bad smell.

It is this revulsion from his world that helps makes sense of his religious and his poetic commitment. Just as the poet converted to Catholicism because he sought the real presence of the divine in the bread and wine of the sacrament of Communion, so too does his poetry seek to repeat such a transforming act of assimilation. The priest's performative act in the climax of the Mass is a verbal one but the words make the bread and wine become, ontologically not symbolically, the body and blood of Christ. Hopkins' religious conversion was the act of someone seeking a confirmation of Being that was seen to be lacking in Protestantism.

Hopkins' religiosity can be a vexation for non-believers, or non-Christian believers, who want to enjoy reading the poetry without feeling that in some way their different beliefs interfere with or in some way dilute the quality of the reading experience. It may be felt that while the deep religious impulse of the poet can be readily acknowledged, this cannot be then simply bracketed off in the hope that it will somehow go away and stop interfering with the poetry. The poems not only explicitly use religious language, they embody theological ideas and convictions that for the poet go to the very heart of the meaning of the poetry. Faced with this fact, the secular reader seeks a way of bridging what seems to be an abyss of incommensurability. Hopkins, of course, is not unique in this respect and writers as different as Milton, Spinoza and Kierkegaard all have religious ideas at the heart of their great texts. It is also true that for these three writers their understanding of God is so radically different from one another that the concept can be interpreted in all sorts of ways and need not be seen as a barrier to understanding or appreciation. The idea of God can be understood in different ways and at different levels. Metaphorically, God can be understood as a mode of interiority – in the sense that Derrida is getting at when he writes of God in Kierkegaard as "the name of the possibility I have of keeping a secret that is visible from the interior but not from the exterior." Or, to put the idea of God in another way, the divine can be conceived as an expression of the realisation that the world is independent of our individual will. Metaphysically, God could be an expression of the feeling that there is more to being alive than material existence. On an existential level, religious experience could be an act of making known one's self, conversing with one's consciousness and engaging with the self through prayer in an attempt to transcend mere bodily existence. The religious impulse can be viewed in terms of a self-reflective need for fullness and an intact sense of self, incorporating individual subjectivities but without diminishing their value because of the way they are seen as part of a larger, affirmative totality. In ways like these, God may be a vehicle – though not the particular model many would choose for themselves – for the creation of ethical values.

What can be seen to follow from these ways of understanding God – all of which help us to understand what Hopkins understood by God – is that Hopkins' religion is inseparable from the passion of his thought and from his intellectual and emotional response to existence. What matters is the depth of feeling and intellect in his writing and whether the reader, warming to what is being addressed, is able to respect and be stimulated by the writer's response. As the opening two stanzas of 'The Wreck of the Deutschland' make clear, Hopkins' endeavour to find and anchor his sense of self in the way that he did was not easily achieved. He experienced his own mental storm and shipwreck and emerged intact – "I did say yes" – discovering a way of living alongside God ("For I greet him the days I meet him, and bless when I understand") and responding to the circuit of Being so that his self is bound up with a divine force of love and energy that gives significance to existence. What Hopkins and others call the mystery of faith is the realisation that this level of meaning is there to be experienced ("instressed, stressed") but not capable of being made rational.

It helps to bear in mind this description of Hopkins by an anonymous Jesuit contemporary:

> What struck me most of all in him was his child-like guilelessness and simplicity ... Joined to this and closely connected with it, was his purity of heart ... he had a distinct dash of genius. His opinion on any subject in heaven and earth was always fresh and original ... If I had known him outside [the Jesuit order], I should have said that his love of speculation and originality of thought would make it almost impossible for him to submit his intellect to authority.

It is the expression of these admirable and singular qualities in his poetry that matters; what is important is the fact that in expressing them the religious language that is very often employed is not necessarily a non-negotiable barrier. When an expression or image is found wanting – where lines in a poem fail to satisfy – it is worth asking if the fault lies in the nature and suggestiveness of the image itself rather than in the explicitly religious language being used. The last two lines of 'God's Grandeur':

> Because the Holy Ghost over the bent
> World broods with warm breast and with ah! bright wings.

fail to chime with the excitement of what has gone before, not principally because a theological explanation is being offered but because the somewhat infelicitous image of an oversized bird brooding solicitously over the world does not carry the intended sense of nature's reassuring, cyclical renewal. The lines fail to perform. There is a similar kind of problem with the last three lines of 'The Starlight Night':

> These are indeed the barn; withindoors house
> The shocks. This piece-bright paling shuts the spouse
> Christ home, Christ and his mother and all his hallows.

where the imagery strains awkwardly to assert a customary piety rather than display a felt experience. The concluding lines of 'The Lantern out of Doors' also express a conventional piety but this time they do not jar with what has gone before:

> Christ minds: Christ's interest, what to avow or amend
> There, éyes them, heart wánts, care haúnts, foot fóllows kínd,
> Their ránsom, théir rescue, ánd first, fást, last friénd.

The poignancy of the poet's aloneness is felt throughout and the poem's final theological comfort, far from ringing false or sounding authoritarian, is experienced as a longed-for statement of value in a lonely universe. Worthwhile human contact, needing physical proximity, is thwarted by separation and loss, and the painful sense of vulnerability that pervades the poem is held together through the imagery of light and dark and metaphors of commercial gain, loss and hoped-for equity. People matter, says the poem, relationships where a chord is struck make a difference, and the poet holds on preciously to this redeeming truth.

2

Poems of Inscape and Instress

After writing 'The Wreck of the Deutschland' in 1875, despite
its unenthusiastic reception which resulted in the poem not being
published, Hopkins felt released to write poetry and he pours
out his heart in celebration of the natural world. 'God's
Grandeur', 'The Starlight Night' and 'Spring', written in the
spring and summer of 1877, deliciously announce Hopkins'
distinctive signature. All three are standard sonnets with a
conventional rhyme scheme, so in one sense there is little here
of that stylistically audacious manner that will come to be seen
as a hallmark of the poet. Nonetheless, there is something keenly
emotional about the mimetic, ebullient language and the
gorgeously precise descriptions, and there is no mistaking the
highly sensuous charge that informs the poems:

> What is all this juice and all this joy?
>   A strain of the earth's sweet being in the beginning
> In Eden garden. – Have, get, before it cloy,

'Pied Beauty', written later in the same year, is better at
conveying the wilful unorthodoxy of Hopkins' spiritual and
poetic relationship with the world. The poem is a flawless
example of Hopkins' philosophy of harmony through difference:
the rhyming of the world is like the resonance of musical
harmony which is like the rhyming of sounds. Piedness is a
manifestation of this relationship, one that needs difference to
be what it is. A dappled sky, like a brinded cow, a trout, a chestnut
or the wing of a finch, possess their individual identities while

at the same time sharing something, just as "swift, slow; sweet, sour; adazzle, dim" are oxymorons yet alike in sound. Fields are all fields yet they come in a variety of shapes and sizes for if all were exactly alike both the world and the word 'field', for example, would be diminished in meaning. Of course he actually says "Landscape plotted and pieced – fold, fallow, and plough". He relishes non-competitive variety for its own sake and celebrates what is not uniform, synonymous, predictable or profitable. All is movement and activity, everything is being itself – "spare" and "strange" – but the result of all this piedness is not experienced as a mindless, random flux, on the contrary it is "past change", and beauty is beauty because of its multicoloured, symphonic variety.

Going beyond just sensuous enjoyment of nature's variety in these poems, Hopkins joins creativity ("All things counter, original, spare, strange") – of which 'Pied Beauty' is a part – with the contemplation of what transcends the utilitarian. Nature is not a means to an end, and self-expression comes from the realisation and enjoyment of this, from feeling at home in a natural world which Hopkins experiences aesthetically much more than he does intellectually. His love of Duns Scotus arose from the philosopher's argument that the aesthetic and the intellectual are complementary modes of authenticating the world and this is the metaphysic of the poem. The being of the world is predicated upon difference but not one that threatens to collapse into a discontinuous sea of signifiers. Dappledness and stippleness form the principle that structures relationships built upon dissimilarity – "Whatever is fickle, freckled (who knows how?)".

Hopkins, so aware and appreciative of the beauty of the world, could not help but also be aware of how industrialisation was disfiguring the physical landscape. Travels around Britain, sojourns in cities and exposure there to working-class life would open his eyes to the cultural as well as the ecological damage of capitalism. His letter about communism is sometimes regarded as an aberration on his part and yet, ten years later, Hopkins writes how his life in Liverpool and Glasgow "laid upon my mind a conviction, a truly crushing conviction, of the misery of town life to the poor and more than to the poor ... of the hollowness of this century's civilisation: it made even life a burden to me to have daily thrust upon me the things I saw." This is anticipated in 'God's Grandeur':

> And all is seared with trade; bleared, smeared with toil;
> And wears man's smudge and shares man's smell: the soil
> Is bare now, nor can foot feel, being shod.

where the trudging rhythm and the heavy, repetitive stresses capture the wearing down of the human spirit through utilitarianism, just as the internal rhyme and onomatopoeic weariness of "seared ... smeared ... smudge" reduces the quality of man's activity to one of unfeeling joylessness. What has been lost is what 'Pied Beauty' celebrates, relating to nature in a way that is not exploitative, not merely satisfying a need, a way that encompasses "all trades, their gear and tackle and trim" as part of nature instead of trade as a cause of pain and pollution ('sears') to nature.

Dealing with just such issues, 'The Caged Skylark' is a sustained and tautly-argued poetic disquisition about what is in the present and what is possible in the future. The simile of the opening lines:

> As a dare-gale skylark scanted in a dull cage
> Man's mounting spirit in his bone-house, mean house,
> dwells –

captures succinctly this dichotomy by contrasting the courageous spirit of a free being with its physical incarceration, mirroring the soulless drudgery of man's estranged existence with the bird's "beyond the remembering" of its former life. The next four lines maintain seamlessly the similarities: both occasionally sing sweetly and both sometimes rail in anger against their plight. Resolution, for a non-believer at least, is not by way of refuge in some other world – "Man's spirit will be flesh-bound when found at best" – but in the possibility of enlightened change into a better world.

A skylark is central to another poem of this period, 'The Sea and the Skylark', one that makes clear that such ideas and emotions are not those of a posed, impersonal mood of weary resignation, mere middle-class ennui. The poem is the result of a week's visit to Rhyl, a seaside town that attracted the exhausted, labouring classes of Liverpool and Manchester when they had some holiday time but which, far from being able to change their condition, only drew attention to the baneful culture that robbed them of life's possibilities. The octave celebrates a medley of natural movement and sound by way of characterising life's richness and rich potential. The to-and-fro motion of the sea happily coexists with the up-and-down movement of the lark, while in turn the ascending lark counterpoints the downwards unreeling of its gleeful song:

> … I hear the lark ascend,
> His rash-fresh re-winded new-skeinèd score
> In crisps of curl off wild winch whirl, and pour
> And pelt music, till none's to spill nor spend.

All this only serves to shame the debased culture of the town, provoking a desire to withdraw from the human world in disgust. The poem's final, depressing thought – "down/To man's last dust, drain fast towards man's first slime." – is a draining-down of life's possibilities to its unfulfilled Darwinian origins.

Such negative thoughts are not characteristic of the 1877 poems and it is the last one he wrote before leaving Wales for good, 'Hurrahing in Harvest', that serves best to remind us of the joy in living that Hopkins experienced so intensely for a brief period in his life. Although the first person pronoun occurs three times in one line, there is little that is egotistic about the poem because it is a jubilant evocation of a possible relationship between people and nature. Nature is to be appropriated – and this is pure Marx – not in terms of possessing or having but in an aesthetic and sensuous form that is emancipatory. People can be satisfied, deeply and sensuously so, to the point of being themselves and expressing their selves, in nature and as a part of it. This, in a way, is what Hopkins is doing when he humanises nature in the poem: beauty is "barbarous", the wind "walks" in the sky and the clouds, fusing noun and adjective in an astonishingly tactile way that suggests texture, fragility and shape, are "silk-sack". The wealth of nature and the wealth of human activity is capable of fusing the objective (nature as something external) and the subjective (people creatively using nature) in a way that for Hopkins finds expression in an innocent sexuality:

> ... what lips yet gave you a
> Rapturous love's greeting of realer, of rounder replies?

The looking self bridges sky and earth and is rewarded in a movement of Being's reciprocity that, like the principle of unity behind the dappled and stippled flux of 'Pied Beauty', sees order in anarchy. The stooks of corn are barbarous, the wind moves randomly, clouds mould themselves into shapes before melting into the sky – what could all be just pleasing chaos is made meaningful by the circle of communication that brings the self and the world together. The equine metaphor that sustains the sestet of 'Hurrahing in Harvest' – "as a stallion stalwart, very – violet-sweet!" – gives expression to the epiphany of mutual understanding and movement that comes from positing the self inside nature. The metaphor is a strange one, carried safely along in the reassuring alliteration of "stallion", "stalwart" and "sweet" but, with "very-violet-sweet" hovering on the edge of very *violent* sweet, suggesting the tender and vulnerable at the very least. The final image rears up literally and figuratively, a burst of purposeful joy that maintains the buoyancy and conviction of this paean to rural life and labour.

It is very evident from poems like 'Hurrahing in Harvest'

that there is a tension between, on the one hand, a sensuous and mimetic use of language and, on the other, a finely wrought, intellectual sense of design. A sacramental celebration of natural beauty is merged with the propositional and controlled form of the sonnet. In the three sonnets of 1877, the transition from descriptive octave to the theological sestet is quite transparent but with 'The Windhover', written in the same year, there is a fusing of sound and sense that carries the poem to a higher level. By way of approaching 'The Windhover', consider this extract from a letter Hopkins wrote to Coventry Patmore, criticising him and others for the nature of their prose:

> At bottom what you do is to think aloud, to think with pen and paper ... Each thought is told off singly and there follows a pause and this breaks the continuity, the strain of address which writing should usually have. The beauty, the eloquence, of good prose, cannot come wholly from the thought.

The insistence that good prose is not just an expression of thought is a reminder of what Hopkins found in Duns Scotus and Parmenides – the primacy of being, and intuition rather than rationality as a way of acquiring knowledge of this. Language itself can become a kind of sensation, akin to some vague bodily feeling, that naturally lends itself to metaphor when it attempts to prise open and reveal some aspect of the world. The mere verbal expression of a thought is inadequate because it fails to enact the ontological quality of what is being described. In this sense, 'The Windhover' aspires to be a performative act; Hopkins wants the words to bring into existence for the reader the very thing that the propositional content of the poem (the kestrel's flight) describes. Hence the power and asyndetic density of the octave where lines are crowded with single, intensive words and where the incessant activity of the bird is mimed by the tense exclamatory pace that creates the breathless excitement of the observer. The term observer, though, is too detached and empirical a word for someone who cannot remain impartial in face of the whirling, theatrical movement of bird and air.

The first four and a half lines enact the kestrel's upwards flight and use of wing movement as a rein to control and thus ride the wind by hovering in the air. The exclamatory "I caught" and the run of three *m's* in "this morning morning's minion" imitates the smooth progression of aerial movement; the stress pattern – with the stronger stress of "morning's" creating a slight pause between the other two words – miming the motion of lifting and pausing before bringing the rising movement to a momentary halt with the abrupt stress of "king-". In the next line, the image of the "dapple-dawn-drawn Falcon" could be suggesting the etched outline of the bird against the backdrop of the sky but the more kinetic impression is that of the bird being drawn upwards towards the dappled early morning sky. The air is in movement, rolling beneath it, but it seems level and steady such is the finesse of the kestrel's responses to changes in air pressure. There is pressure too in the suggestiveness of the word "rung", the reining of a horse to direct its movement and the felt pressure of resistance in the hand holding the reins, while the image of a skate's heel's turn on a bow-bend captures the easy physical grace of a body in motion banking against the curve of its climb.

The ambiguous "Buckle!" (perhaps no single word of poetry has been so discussed and interpreted and seen as absolutely vital to a poem's whole meaning) signifies the moment of instress when knowledge is experienced as an *imm*ediacy, not mediated, an experience of *app*rehension and *com*prehension. "Buckle", as a verb, a doing word, comes after a series of nouns, and grammar leads us to expect that the verb's meaning relates back to some quality of doing shared by the nouns "Brute beauty", "valour", aerial action, pride and plumage. Or perhaps it is the very sharing and combining of the nouns' qualities that lies behind the choice of the word buckle, as in the coming together of two sides of a belt when it is buckled. At the same time, though, the poem's last three lines invite us to see a connection; a link between the meaning of this doing word "Buckle" and the doing that is going on with the plough's activity and the embers' activity. What they both do is yield, open up to view, something that is only revealed in their activity: the shining of a sod of earth opened up by the straight edge of the plough in a sillion (or – an alternative reading of this image – the shining of the plough-share itself through its activity of rubbing against the sods of earth), and the coruscating glow of the embers in their final act of falling apart. Putting these possible readings of "Buckle" together, the word suggests a yielding, a showing forth as the result of a coming together of the temporal attributes in a moment of sublation that is also a revelation. What is yielded up is the essential nature, the very being itself, of the falcon, but when the verb is read and heard as an imperative and not an indicative it is also calling attention to and proclaiming its existence. This, we recall, is the idea in 'As kingfishers catch fire, dragonflies draw flame' that being and doing are not separate for through activity being is realised. "*What I do is me: for that I came*" cries the kestrel. "Buckle!", then, is the pivotal moment of experience when what is encountered is the inner energy that upholds the distinctive pattern of a being's individuality. It is the moment of recognising and seeing into what in a letter Hopkins called a thing's "sake", "that in the thing by virtue of which especially it has [its] being abroad".

What is witnessed in the kestrel's flight is unique but there is also the communal possibility of an experience that is open to anyone, just as it is to Hopkins with his "heart in hiding". The poem and its excited energy and mimetic word-power can be experienced as a call upon the reader to catch her own "morning's minion", the selfness that binds being, by seizing what is one's own, managing currents every which way, riding bows and bends in the sheer doing of what one has the ability or talent to do. Only then might there come that moment of blissful self-realisation which is also a moment of danger if one is to take the existential risk of committing the whole self to one's chosen purpose and pathway through life – "AND the fire that breaks from thee then, a billion/Times told lovelier, more dangerous, O my chevalier!" – a line of thought that takes in "Buckle!" as an arming for battle and engagement in close combat. Here and elsewhere, the poem's references to chivalry and knightly endeavour can be interpreted in terms of Christian iconography but the medievalism is just as meaningful in existential terms of the struggle to be authentic to one's sense of self, the nobility of the challenge and the dangers attendant upon taking up the challenge. The ending of the poem, after all, is not one of quietism for it is only the sheer effort of driving the plough that causes the bright shine and the embers only give off their brightest glow when they break away from the all-consuming fire and "Fall, gall themselves" against the outer world. Just as the poem ends on a high note with the vividly realised flash of "gold-vermilion", and just as the poet finds his spirits roused and enlivened by what he sees, the reader is left enthused by Hopkins' own exuberant spirit at witnessing a life lived to the full.

The particular fame of 'The Windhover' encourages a view of Hopkins as a nature poet at the expense of other fine poems he wrote where the subject is a person or a place. 'The Bugler's First Communion' was written two years later and displays a delicacy of touch and an intimacy that is all the more moving when one considers the reality of soldiers' life in a barracks. Hopkins was not unaware of the kind of crudity and coarseness that would have characterised life at the Crowley Barracks where he was called upon to carry out priestly duties although, as the far less impressive poem 'The Soldier, shows, he was not immune to Victorian chauvinism and the era's penchant for glorifying the army as the preserve of national manhood and virtues. 'The Bugler's First Communion' is not in any way facile or sentimentally romantic and, indeed, the poem gains its integrity *because* the poet knows very well the kind of temptations awaiting the tender young bugler. He fears for the soldier, seeks to lock up safely everything that is gracious about him, and the gentle vehemence of the final stanzas bear witness to his fretful concerns. The syntax and vocabulary strains to make itself understood in places as Hopkins works hard, perhaps too hard, to craft an original poem that will do justice to his mixed feelings of holy joy and human trepidation. When the reader has wrestled with the difficult lines and images – all available annotations and textual commentaries need consulting – and the poem is again read aloud as a whole then it is very likely to succeed and impress. The success of 'The Bugler's First Communion' is due to the way its unlikely blend of elements work together without jarring. The occasion is a deeply religious one for the poet priest, he is administering Holy Communion: one wafer of bread which has become for him the body of the divine, is taken from its tabernacle and placed on the tongue of the worshipper. While preserving the sanctity of the moment he earnestly and devotedly offers up a prayer in an innovative poetic form that combines rich natural imagery in a tone that seeks to be relaxed and colloquial, at the same time admitting to very real misgivings about the future of a young man about to be shipped off to the Punjab at the risk of his life and soul. The poem gives us a rare glimpse into the sacred side of Hopkins' working life and the purity of his vocation shines through.

In 'Harry Ploughman' and 'Tom's Garland' two other individuals, a ploughman and an unemployed labourer, also come to life and are realised in their labour; and their labour is the source and being of the dignity they possess. This is what Hopkins meant when he said of 'Harry Ploughman' that the only criterion for judging the poem was the degree to which it made Harry a vivid figure. Any vividness attaching to the farmer is a function of the dignity and grace that comes from the man at work. The poem, an almost baroque example of Hopkins' elliptical style with unexpected juxtapositions and a preference for caesura in place of conjunctions and prepositions, is just about saved from the charge of technical over-wroughtness by the lavish play of words aestheticising the male body. The poet digs deep, Heaney-style, for words of ancient meaning ("broth", "curded", "Churlsgrace") and the reader requires the aid of an annotated text to make semantic sense of the farmer's muscular power primed to release the invisible horses and set in motion both the action of the plough and the machine's demands on the body as the ploughman runs alongside the churned-up clods of earth. The poem, a tremendous achievement of verbal sculpture in the way it renders the visceral, possesses a language that is as muscular and sinewy as Harry himself.

'Tom's Garland' is a more tangled composition although the basic argument of the poem (a variation on the theme of what he had said many years earlier in his letter to Bridges about being a sort of communist) is not difficult to follow, thanks to Hopkins' own explanation. Tom, the ring of steel around whose boots form the garland of the title, and his fellow-worker Dick have finished a hard day's work. Sparks fly from the contact of Dick's boots with the ground as they trudge homewards. Tom is a navvy, an unskilled labourer who is now thinking only of his supper and the good night's sleep that will follow his meal. Although his lot is a hard one, he is a healthy and strong worker who does not dwell on matters political, unquiet thoughts that could prick his composure, for he senses that even in a more equal society he would still be the same kind of person labouring in much the same way. It is enough for Tom to be alive and well and he cares not for degrees of rank and status. But, and here's the rub, not everyone in his world is able to find satisfaction and self-worth and there are those who are neither at the top of the social scale, enjoying prestige, or more lowly placed but with the dignity of their labour. The dispossessed, the unemployed, have nothing and are deprived of the pleasure that comes from having a place in society. Such a state can lead to despair and laziness but it can also become anger and rage at the inequality that robs them of dignity and self-respect. Such anger is capable of gripping the whole class of the exploited, turning them into a revolutionary mob intent on mayhem. The poem itself, though, lacks ease; the portrayal of "sturdy Dick" and "Tom Heart-at-ease" verges on the patronising; there is something patrician and feudal-like about the ideal of the well-ordered and organic commonwealth where everyone from lord to labourer is happy with their station; and the final lines are inadequate in their sensationalism.

'Felix Randal' is concerned with the sense of dignity through labour but is all the stronger for its absence of ideology and the melancholic ache that underlies its contrast between the feebleness of the dying blacksmith and the memory of what had once been:

> How far from then forethought of, all thy more boisterous
>   years,
> When thou at the random grim forge, powerful amidst peers,
> Didst fettle for the great grey drayhorse his bright and battering
>   sandal!

The single word "boisterous" is rich in its connotations, suggesting a fullness of being, a lively unmediated enjoyment of life that is inseparable from the vivid picture of the blacksmith at work. We see him in his world, realising himself through his labour and forging his social identity amidst his peers – the poem's phrase is the natural one to use – just as surely as the horseshoe he makes ready for the drayhorse. It is a world the reader can readily believe in, far more so than any of the worlds imagined in 'Tom's Garland', one that is constituted by the use of words like "random" (a technical term meaning rough stonework but also suggesting the cluttered order of the work-place) and "drayhorse" and "fettle", and a colloquial tone that accompanies the enjambment that is a feature of the poem. The forge is as much a part of the blacksmith's existence as the air and sky is to the windhover's and both poems bring expression and emotion together in a perfectly complementary pitch. Compassionate tenderness marks the mood of the poem and the contrast between "child, Felix, poor Felix Randal" and the once "big-boned and hardy-handsome" craftsman evokes the same kind of sadness at human mortality that characterises another poem, 'Spring and Fall'. At another level, the reader cannot help but contrast this vignette of Hopkins caring for the sick and fulfilling his own work in a deeply meaningful way with the later Hopkins who will become tortured with unhappiness in the final years of his existence in Dublin.

The felt happiness that is so discernible in the poems written in Wales became increasingly muted in the years that followed and his posting to a church in Liverpool in 1880 signals a realisation on his part that he has neither the time, energy nor conviction to compose verse. The period after leaving Wales and leading up to Liverpool, the most "museless" of places he calls it, and the time after it up until his posting to Dublin in 1884 is marked not by a series of poems but by sporadic compositions arising from or provoked by contingencies. The first of these, 'The Loss of the Eurydice', has moments of interest and verve but as a whole the poem fails to engage with many readers. As a poem about a shipwreck and the loss of innocent lives it inevitably invites comparison with 'The Wreck of the Deutschland' and Bridges was in no doubt about his preference for 'The Loss of the Eurydice', praising it inordinately. Two others from the small circle of Hopkins' acquaintances who read the poem were also genuinely impressed by the composition and it was only *The Month*, the official Jesuit journal, which turned it down for publication just as it had rejected Hopkins' first poem about a shipwreck. The probable reasons underlying Bridges' praise of the poem are now, justifiably, seen as its weaknesses. The poem concedes far too much to the unfolding of what happened and is capable of being summarised; unlike 'The Wreck of the Deutschland' where a need for a paraphrase falls away as a distraction. The narrative of 'The Loss of the Eurydice' closely follows the actual course of events that led to the sinking of a training ship suddenly overturned by an unforeseen squall and the loss of all but two of those aboard the vessel. The concluding four stanzas of the poem seem narrowly doctrinal and the poem is peppered with conventional pieties, with the one potentially interesting reference to Duns Scotus left undeveloped: "And one – but let be, let be:/More, more than was will yet be".

As Hopkins spends more time in urban environments, near Sheffield, London, Oxford for nearly a year, then Lancashire, it is the passing away of the beauty of being that registers a key note in the better poems of this period. As well as 'The Bugler's First Communion' and 'Felix Randal', the poems that distinguish themselves are 'Spring and Fall', 'Henry Purcell', 'The Candle Indoors', 'As kingfishers catch fire, dragonflies draw flame' and 'Ribblesdale'. There is also 'Binsey Poplars', where once again Hopkins assertively proclaims, albeit it negatively, the ontological energy of being, and 'Duns Scotus's Oxford' where there is an intensely wistful recreation of the city's inscape and instress:

> Towery city and branchy between towers;
> Cuckoo-echoing, bell-swarmèd, lark-charmèd, rook-racked,
>   river-rounded

'Ribblesdale' is a worrying poem in more than one way. In it Hopkins frets about people's grudging appreciation of natural beauty but he does so in an almost cynical, misanthropic way, ruefully accepting that the fate of the rugged beauty of the Lancashire moorland is doomed to remain unloved. The last six lines of the poem return to what was first noted in 'God's Grandeur', the threat to man's metaphysical relationship with being posed by soulless commerce ("so tied to his turn") and an exploitative attitude ("thriftless reave") towards what should be experienced as an organic whole:

> And what is Earth's eye, tongue, or heart else, where
> Else, but in dear and dogged man? – Ah, the heir
> To his own selfbent so bound, so tied to his turn,

To thriftless reave both our rich round world bare
And none reck of world after, this bids wear
Earth brows of such care, care and dear concern.

Worrying for the reader, too, is the realisation that the poet himself seems to lack passionate engagement with the natural scene. He tells us what is wrong but is unable himself to experience what should be possible and Ribblesdale as a particular place with its own inscape evades the poet's grasp.

It is difficult to know where best to place and approach 'The Wreck of the Deutschland' and Bridges was right for once when he said that it stood like a dragon at the gates of Hopkins' poetry. It is a complex poem where the contradictory and contentious mix of emotions – joy, masochism, violence, resignation, depression, disenchantment, exaltation and desperate ecstasy – is inseparable from the invigorating language dramatising the poet's anguished confrontation with the mystery of existence. States of nature are as contrary as the turmoil of human emotions, so that literal and metaphorical descriptions of land- and sea-scapes become difficult to disentangle. The fierce storm ("Sitting Eastnortheast, in cursed quarter") unleashes forces of nature that endanger mental as well as physical survival and this shapes itself into a theme of the poem. The experience of personal angst in Part I, is described in metaphors of fire, water and sand, is consciously echoed in the physical force of lightning and ocean power that overwhelms the ship.

Yet there is also the placid loveliness of a divinely-inspired nature that warrants applause ("Kiss my hand to the dappled-with-damson west"). Striving for a balance, seeking a settlement between the terror of a punishing deity ("The frown of his face/ Before me, the hurtle of hell/Behind") and an ultimately divine justice, the chances of successfully unifying such contraries, or just accepting a resolution of some kind, seems a demanding task doomed to fail; and both at a poetic and a metaphysical level 'The Wreck of the Deutschland' falls short of achieving its intention. The urged-for religious nationalism of the final stanza, the resurrection and salvation, is lovingly evoked ("Let him easter in us") but never convinces and at this doctrinal level the poem fails just as the unresolved tensions of language remain knotted. In the originality of its poetic form, however, and in the intensity of expression the poem is a remarkable success, even if readers are likely to recall and remain moved by individual stanzas and patterns of sound rather than the poem as an organic and satisfying whole.

Part I is written as the result of the shipwreck but instead of being the poem's conclusion it inaugurates its beginning, climaxing with an audacious simile that supposedly expresses religious fervour but which bursts orgasmically like the plum itself:

> ... How a lush-kept plush-capped sloe
> Will, mouthed to flesh-burst,
> Gush! – flush the man, the being with it, sour or sweet,
> Brim, in a flash, full! ...

The rhyming of "lush" and "plush", signalling the ripe potential that is protected ("-capped") and untapped ("-kept"), slips into "gush" and "flush" as sensuous separateness collapses in a moment of charged sexuality.

The poem as a whole displays a remarkable degree of metrical control and a startling precision of imagery:

> 'Some find me a sword; some
> The flange and the rail; flame,
> Fang, or flood' goes Death on drum,
> And storms bugle his fame.
> But wé dream we are rooted in earth – Dust!
> Flesh falls within sight of us, we, though our flower the same,
> Wave with the meadow, forget that there must
> The sour scythe cringe, and the blear share come.

In this, the opening stanza of Part II, the grim reaper appears as a terrifying shape-shifter, marching fatalistically to the sound of a drum. The sprung rhythm actualises the beat of the drum –

"The fláñge and the ráil; fláme,/Fáñg, or flood" – and a storm that is metaphysical as much as meteorological blares out like a bugle. The harshness of the reality of death reduces our fond illusions to dust and our precious self-identity, robbed of its subjectivity, becomes the insubstantial 'flesh' of a Hieronymus Bosch painting. The caper of being alive, a beguiling dance with an appearance of harmony, is nothing more than a medieval Dance of Death, a mere motion of waving that will succumb to the metallic slaughter that begins and ends the stanza.

What follows in Part II, the description of the storm and shipwreck, is a tortured struggle with meaning as the untamed sea and its unfocused, repetitive motion becomes the theatre for the world's resistance to significance. The language enacts this struggle but in the end the struggle for meaning in the poem is too urgent and too violently changeable to suggest an easy victory on any side. Stanza 21, for example, moves from comfortable lyricism ("Banned by the land of their birth,/Rhine refused them, Thames would ruin them;") to surreal trans-formations ("Storm flakes were scroll-leaved flowers, lily showers – sweet/heaven was astrew in them") as if we are not supposed to notice such a dislocation within a stanza. Stanza 22 anxiously but absolutely insists on a set of signs – "cipher", "mark", "scores it", "stigma", "signal", "token" – that will be more than mere signifiers. Insistence on a deep significance is not the same, however, as enactment or even persuasion, and the contortions of language in Part II leave us flustered at times. Hopkins addresses the divine as a force that reconciles opposites – "Thou art lightning and love, I found it, a winter and warm" – but such contraries are not so easily unified for many readers of the poem. As will be looked at later, the heady play with language and complexities of rhythm that weave their way through the tapestry of the poem makes the poem a sitting target for the post-structuralist school of literary criticism.

3

A Stranger in a Strange Land

The conviction that enabled Hopkins to make sense of his life and poetry came from his realisation that being and doing are not separate and that through activity being is realised. His own being, as a priest and poet, would realise itself through his work as a Jesuit and through his poetry. Hopkins became desperately unhappy in Ireland because he felt he couldn't *be* himself in that environment. Becoming a Professor of Greek at the fledgling University College, Dublin, early in 1884, carried none of the kudos that today one might associate with such a position and, while Hopkins was certainly not seeking prestige and perks, he wanted more from his working life than unrewarding teaching assignments and an unremitting gruel of examination papers to mark at 86 St Stephen's Green. Dublin in the 1880s was a highly politicised city, insular and rebellious and the centre of the country's cultural and political nationalism. Hopkins, although he was not indifferent to Ireland's plight, was an outsider and found it difficult to sympathise with the social, cultural and political conflicts that underlay Irish life.

The problem went deeper than job dissatisfaction and culture shock because his day-to-day work was inseparable from his life as a Jesuit. What was at stake was his spiritual vocation because his work was his profession and his career was as bound up with a sense of identity and self-worth as for anyone whose job becomes the central focus of their life. His Jesuit colleagues only saw the symptoms of his malaise, a lassitude and eccentricity that to them signalled a lack of resolve and commitment to the task of building a Catholic university, and their sympathy was in short supply. Hopkins made some attempt to share his poetry and a fellow professor is supposed to have dismissed them: "Now look here! What you're bringing me isn't poetry at all."

His unsatisfying existence in Dublin brought on a depression that caused Hopkins to examine and assess his life and to ask himself to what extent he had fulfilled his own being, his own self: "That taste of myself, of I and *me* above and in all things, which is more distinctive than the taste of ale or alum, more distinctive than the smell of walnut leaf or camphor." The selfhood that proclaimed itself in 'As kingfishers catch fire, dragonflies draw flame' – "*What I do is me: for that I came*" – became a wryly bitter epitaph to accompany the sense of rupture and lack of self that he felt characterised his existence in Ireland. In 1887 he summed up his period of time in Dublin as "three hard wearying wasting wasted years". He dreams of living on a farm in the west of Ireland but in real life, in the decompression chamber of hyper-politicised Dublin where he is out of place and out of time, a painful and joyless sense of alienation takes root. The result is a series of poems that register varying degrees of somatic distress and spiritual grief. The year 1885-86, like that of 1877, produces a remarkable set of poems, though ones expressing a very different range of feelings.

It is possible to view the connection between Hopkins' move to Dublin and his deep despair solely in terms of cause and effect, surmising that if only the Jesuit order had moved him somewhere more congenial then all would have been well. This is too simplistic and it ignores the less-than-happy thoughts and feelings that are expressed in some of the poems written before he ever boarded the boat for Ireland. It ignores unresolved tensions that are discernible in 'The Wreck of the Deutschland' and the personal sense, associated with his growing feeling of impotence and inability to ever finish anything, that his whole life was a wreck of another kind. The substance of this feeling is detailed in biographies of Hopkins that record the various ventures and scholarly ideas that he became interested in, and drew up plans and preliminary research for, only to find them thwarted by pressure of work and what seems like a psychological inclination to find excuses for not completing projects. "And there they lie and my old notebooks and beginnings of things, ever so many ... ruins and wrecks", he wrote in a late letter. Hopkins, always a stranger in a strange land, was never at ease with his world. The deeply-rooted alienation from Victorian values that motivated his conversion to Catholicism also made itself felt in his inability to compose the kind of attractive but mediocre verse that would earn his friend Bridges a laureateship.

Started in October 1884, 'Spelt from Sibyl's Leaves' is an extraordinary poem, utterly modern and profoundly un-Victorian. The orchestration of sounds at the beginning of the sonnet – "the longest sonnet ever made", claimed Hopkins with some justification – builds up an inexorable sense of the whole earth in a state of momentous movement towards something portentous:

> Earnest, earthless, equal, attuneable, vaulty, voluminous, ... stupendous
> Evening strains to be time's vast, womb-of-all, home-of-all, hearse-of-all night.

The solemnity ("earnest") of the evening is coupled with the other-worldly ("earthless") and the etherealising; the arrival of dusk heralding some kind of tranquillising but unknown and awe-ful presence – pondered in the silence of the dots in line 1 – a sense of infinite time taking possession of the evening sky. The movement of the earth's architecture continues in the third line but the straining tension and the compound adjectives of the first two lines give way to a lighter, alleviating sense of motion in equilibrium, balancing the tender ("fond") flush of the departing sunset ("hornlight") against a less inviting ("wild hollow"), nebulous glow that fills the sky and hangs there, the verse enacting the sense of pausing by coming to rest itself on "height":

> Her fond yellow hornlight wound to the west, her wild
> hollow hoarlight hung to the height

The relaxation is temporary, we are wrenched back to the sense of Doomsday approaching with the abrupt "Waste" at the very start of the fourth line, peremptorily announcing the fading of evening light. What emerges in the night sky is not the impish "fire-folk" of 'The Starlit Night' but a hierarchical order of light as different ranks of light ("her earliest stars, earlstars, stars principal") take up their stations and "overbend" us. The awfulness of what is imminent is starkly announced:

> For earth her being has unbound; her
> dapple is at end,

In 'Pied Beauty', dappledness was a key that opened the doors of perception but now that mode of being – and the whole philosophy so warmly celebrated in the Welsh poems – has been cancelled; it is done with, past. The kind of inscape and instress that was once to be revelled in has been annihilated and selfhood, "páshed" like the pulping of unresisting fruit, loses its organic relationship with others and becomes asocial in its isolation ("self in self"); the division of octave and sestet dissolving at line seven into one profoundly-felt acknowledgement of an approaching apocalypse:

> Óur évening is over us; óur níght whélms, whélms,
> ánd will end us.
> Only the beakleaved boughs dragonish damask the tool-
> smooth bleak light; black,

The Sibyl at Cumae, as Hopkins well knew, inscribed her prophecies on palm leaves but here leaves' branches inscribe themselves fantastically in the growing darkness of night as colourless steely silhouettes resembling beaks and dragons. Readers of the early 21st century will recognise and confirm the truth of the Sibyl's utterance – this indeed is "Óur tale, O óur oracle!" – and there is no Delphic ambiguity that might allow for alternative readings. Plurality, individuality of being, is to be swept aside by a peremptory of fundamentalism that reduces everything to the axes of evil and good:

> lét life wind
> Off hér once skéined stained véined vaàiety upon, áll on two
>   spools; párt, pen, páck
> Now her áll in twó flocks, twó folds – black, white; right,
>   wrong; reckon but, reck but, mind
> But these two; wáre of a wórld where bút these twó tell, each
>   off the óther;

It is a frightening prophecy of our times, a dire warning ("reck but, mind/But these two") of the danger inherent in a civilisation that cancels plurality and reduces all difference to just one dogmatic, binary opposition. The inevitable consequence of such extremism will be to leave us on the rack of a world without community or comfort ("sheathe- and shelterless"), in a moral freefall, with only ricocheting, self-destructive apprehensions that we ourselves have created:

> Where, selfwrung, selfstrung, sheathe- and shelterless, thóughts
> agaínst thoughts ín groans grínd.

'Spelt from Sibyl's Leaves' is a remarkable achievement and especially deserves a performance in the sense that Hopkins wanted all his poetry and all art to perform:

> [E]very work of art has its own play or performance. The play or performance of a stage play is the playing of it on the boards, the stage: reading it, much more writing it, is not its performance. The performance of a symphony is not the scoring of it however elaborately; it is the in the concert room, by the orchestra, and then and there performance only. A

picture is performed, or performs, when anyone looks at it in the proper and intended light. A house performs when it is now built and lived in. To come nearer: book, play, perform, or are played and performed when they are read.

Hopkins knew well, from studying the genesis of poetry in the performances of ancient Greek drama, that poetry "was originally meant for either singing or reciting" and 'Spelt from Sibyl's Leaves', he said, needed to be "almost sung". In this respect, the poet's metrical markings are a help not a hindrance, right down to that final stress on "grínd" that ends the sonnet and twists the knife in the wound.

Composed in August 1885, and revised two years later, 'Carrion Comfort' is often seen as a poem of despair, even the most despairing of the group known as 'the terrible sonnets' and possibly the one that he described to Bridges in an letter around this time as "written in blood". The poem begins with the aftermath of an awful mental struggle and Hopkins can assert in the first line that, no, he will not feed off the putrefying corpse of Despair ('carrion comfort'). He admits to his tenuous grip on selfhood but vows not to unravel altogether the loose threads that are barely holding him together; he is hanging on to his humanity against the odds. The first quatrain is a powerful and dramatic rendering of self-worth; its core emerging from the thrice-repeated negative of the first two lines and ensconced in their insistent beat. He admits to and confronts the painful and deep puzzlement as to why he should be subjected to such a trauma, expressed in the Biblical picture of his puny self, struggling against a force so much stronger and fierce; a force that moves over and through him with "darksome devouring eyes", beating, thrashing him to a huddled heap on the ground. In farming, threshing is the beating out and separating of the wholesome grain from the chaff, an essential process if the grain is to be planted and yield eventual nourishment, and Hopkins has found refuge in thinking of his ordeal in this way as something purifying and ultimately purposeful. He is able to reflect on and modulate his suffering, no longer viewing it as an act of masochism ("I kissed the rod") but as something gracious in his willing submission, like a courtier kissing the hand of a noble. This gentle interpretation, however, is itself modulated as he dwells on the cost to his own psyche, returning the reader to his plight at the beginning of the poem.

How natural though, given the stark power of the opening quatrain, is the progression of thought and argument in the poem; to what extent is this one of the Dublin poems that he described as coming to him "unbidden and against my will"? Perhaps 'Carrion Comfort' is too influenced by the fact that it may have been first composed while he was at a week-long retreat at Clongowes Wood College; the structure is too crafted, too Jesuitical in its framing. There are four lines of self-willed resolve leading to "But ah"; followed by another quatrain, this time detailing the course of the unequal struggle; then the interrogative of line nine and the affirmative response, concluding with another question in line 12 and the odd, almost self-satisfied ending. Is the sense of control in the ending too sure, is there a sense almost of decorum?

In 'No worst, there is none', however, Hopkins hits rock bottom and stays there; there is no refuge and even the comfort of sleep becomes a form of death in the last line: "Life death does end and each day dies with sleep". To be awake is to be "Pitched past pitch of grief", evoking the hopeless plight of a ship on the verge of being wrecked, to unwillingly share the existential dread that afflicts humanity:

> My cries heave, herds-long; huddle in a main, a chief-
> woe, world-sorrow; on an age-old anvil wince and sing –

The cries of despair "heave" like the involuntary motion of physical sickness, like seasickness, perhaps, for the cattle could be huddled together in a ship in a storm (reinforcing echoes of the physical and mental storm in 'The Wreck of the Deutschland'). The suffering is personal to the narrator but it is the "age-old" suffering of the human condition, the psychic pain of existence, as ancient as the hammering on an anvil. The narrator's suffering can only be understood by those who have also wavered on the brink of complete collapse and who therefore know the futility of proffered remedies:

> O the mind, mind has mountains; cliffs of fall
> Frightful, sheer, no-man-fathomed. Hold them cheap
> May who ne'er hung there.

This is only the most famous, the most Shakespearian, of a series of shifting, startling yet unhistrionic images in the poem that speak for his unfathomable and indefinable depression and the pain of knowing no release from a distraught mental grief.

The opening of 'To seem the stranger' expresses the hopeless double bind that afflicts the poet in Dublin. He feels it is his fate to be seen and experienced as strange by others and now he is in another country where people are, objectively, strangers to him. The sense of an ordeal doubling back on itself is captured in the opening chiasmus, inverting in the second phrase ("my life/Among strangers") the order of the first phrase ("To seem the stranger lies my lot"). It is not just the comfort of social relations that eludes him for he now realises, looking back on his life, that the religion which is his "peace" is also the "parting" that separates him from his family and his country, the source of distress ("[my]sword and strife") within himself and politically within the country of Ireland. The cumulative effect of his worrying and poignant self-pity is a terrible sense of lack, a breakdown in his powers of inscape and instress that leaves his words in a state of redundancy – "to hoard unheard,/Heard unheeded, leaves me a lonely began" – and his own selfhood shrunk to immobility with the doing nature of the verb "began" transformed shockingly into an inert noun signifying utter loneliness. Part of the problem is his knowledge, as he made clear in a letter to Bridges in 1884, that the Jesuits will censor anything he writes ("heaven's baffling ban"). Loneliness, only explicitly mentioned in the last line, inhabits the feeling of alienation expressed in the first line and goes on to haunt the whole poem.

'I wake and feel the fell of dark' is a very different poem and the dissimilarity is heard in the rhythm and registered in the imagery. By way of contrast, the melancholy tone of 'To seem the stranger' is carried on a fairly comfortable flow of iambic pentameters and the syntax takes the reader smoothly from one line to the next. The alliteration and internal rhymes in the three and a half lines that bring that poem to its end are recognised almost comfortingly as the familiar voice of Hopkins, to some extent even working against the expressed sentiments of the poem. The rhythm of 'I wake and feel the fell of dark', by way of contrast, has a rasping quality so that, for instance, while the last iamb of the first line of 'To seem the stranger' ("my life") is conjunctive and links purposefully with what has gone before and after, the equivalent iamb in 'I wake and feel the fell of dark' ("not day") signifies a negative appendage which abruptly ends the line. Elsewhere in the poem as in "I am gall, I am heartburn" or "Selfyeast of spirit a dull dough sours", the iambic pentameters give way to emphatic, full-stopped, self-contained pronouncements that abruptly state the despair possessing Hopkins. The poem's beginning, "I wake", takes up from where 'No worst, there is none ends' and prolongs the agony of being alive. There is a compelling compression to the poem as a whole, not minimalist but getting there, that gives its idiom a thoroughly modern feel.

The imagery in this poem also directly and plainly confronts the awfulness of what the poet is feeling. The hours are "black", not so much from night's lack of light as from the horrible realisation that the angst that prevents him sleeping points to the sense of pointlessness in his whole existence – hours turning into years and the years into his life up to the present. It is a dreadful admission, rendered all the more anguished by the ordinariness of the simile that compares his lonely plight and failure to communicate with the sending of "dead letters" that never reach their intended recipient. The sestet goes beyond this poignancy to the self-lacerating confession that his own self is distasteful to him:

> I am gall, I am heartburn. God's most deep decree
> Bitter would have me taste: my taste was me;

The delight in the sensuous physicality of nature that once so enamoured the poet has turned against him and developed into a physical self-loathing and the whole sestet dwells on medical images of psychiatric illness. If Hopkins were to question the foundations of his religious beliefs, to speculate on the possibility of the notion of God as a cognitive error, such self-examination would surely have its place in 'I wake and feel the fell of dark'. This does not take place. The cries of lamentation addressed to the Divine have failed but while this is inexplicable to Hopkins it does not mean or even suggest for him that God is dead (unlike the post office that allows for all possibilities with its 'gone away' on dead letters) and the poem ends with the realisation of how worse must be the plight of the truly damned in hell. How convincing is this conclusion? Hopkins revised the ending – the final line was originally "Their sweating selves as I am mine, but worse" – presumably moving "as I am mine" to the start of the line to lessen the possibility of a misreading that might allow 'as I am mine, but worse' to suggest the poet's plight is worse than that of the damned. Be that as it may, there remains something lingeringly ambiguous about the conclusion and the consanguineous plight of the poet and the damned remains uppermost. Many readers will draw their own conclusion – that Hopkins is in a living hell and that there is little real comfort in thinking how worse it is for the eternally damned.

'Patience, hard thing!' expresses a more sanguine and intellectual analysis of life, though still a fretful one, exhibiting the literary quality that F.R. Leavis praised as the "stress of cerebral muscle". There is a type of dock plant which is called patience in parts of northern England because its leaves and shoots were used to make a pudding that was eaten during the last two weeks of Lent, the period before Easter traditionally marked by voluntary acts of fasting and deprivation, and which requires a harsh, limeless soil in which to grow. Patience the virtue, says Hopkins, also only grows in a certain soil – "Rare patience roots in these, and, these away [absent],/Nowhere" – and the first five lines of the poem are concerned with the peculiar nature of this human ecology. Its characteristic is passivity, arising from an absence of lively engagement with the world and expressed parenthetically in a martial image ("Wants war, wants wounds"), which requests that one "do without, take tosses, and obey". Such submissive qualities define the nature of patience and constitute its being – "But bid for, Patience is!"

The rest of 'Patience, hard thing!' develops around a strange and intellectually intricate series of metaphors that work together in a surprisingly felicitous way. The gardening image is sustained in a picture of patience as an ivy plant that grows around the human heart but the focus of interpretation has shifted. Patience, seemingly a virtue, now takes on other, almost Freudian, connotations:

> Natural heart's ivy, Patience masks
> Our ruins of wrecked past purposes. There she basks
> Purple eyes and seas of liquid leaves all day.

The virtue becomes a mask, a cover for past failures that are sunk to the bottom of our consciousness, like a wreck, and the ivy becomes a sinister and lurid life form of its own. The momentary warmth of "basks" becomes physical and psychic discomfort as "We hear our hearts grate on themselves", and the next line and a half twists syntax as it wrestles dialectically with the wishful endeavour to fall in line with a higher purpose:

> Yet the rebellious wills
> Of us we do bid God bend to him even so.

In 'I wake and feel the fell of dark', the divine rationale, the bigger picture that would justify and make sense of this strife, "lives alas! away" and here too there is a question about the ultimate purpose. The final metaphor is the benevolent and comforting one of God filling the honeycombs of our existence with patience and in a way that only those who have experienced this ministration can know the truth of: for "that comes those ways we know". The philosophical conclusion in this final image is expressed more convincingly than in the ending of 'I wake and feel the fell of dark', but while we accept the authenticity of the poet's sense of closure the reader may be left instead with the image of human failure lying wrecked at the bottom of a psychological sea.

What is remarkable about 'Patience, hard thing!' is the way in which, as a poem, it enacts an argument or conversation with itself. Patience is at first characterised as a rare virtue, demanding and unheroic but virtuous nonetheless, but this is quickly qualified by the ambiguous implications of the ivy image and the suggestion that what is repressed in the name of patience remains in the mind. What is repressed is not dormant; it is felt and experienced as a terrible vulnerability. Yet, despite or because of this, the mind struggles for contentment – the poem is this struggle – and finally finds release and relief in stoicism.

Another undated poem of this period, 1885-86, 'My own heart let me more have pity on', is also a conversation with the self and it arrives at a similarly hopeful conclusion, though one that rests less on stoicism than on the need to care for one's soul and to be solicitous towards one's own self. It is an easier poem to read than 'Patience, hard thing!', both at the level of syntax and imagery, suggesting a greater resolve to get to grips with depression. The poem avoids self-pity and the opening lines handle the inversion of word order in as controlled and composed a style as the rest of the poem, expressing a gentle self-compassion in the face of what could be an overwhelming cycle of self-inflicted pain:

> My own heart let more have pity on; let
> Me live to my sad self hereafter kind,
> Charitable; not live this tormented mind
> With this tormented mind tormenting yet.

The poem shows Hopkins writing, characteristically, as if English were an inflected language, like the Greek and Latin he knew so well, allowing words to be placed where they work to best effect metrically and dramatically. From his study of classical Greek poetry, Hopkins also knew well how some words could be omitted altogether, their presence being implied. In lines six and seven, for example:

> By groping round my comfortless, than blind
> Eyes in their dark can day or thirst can find

a word like 'mind' (or 'world', as Bridges suggested) after "comfortless" and 'see' after the first "can" are taken as given.

The conversational tone 'My own heart let me more have pity on' – so assured in its informality and common sense advice:

> Soul, self; come poor Jackself, I do advise
> You, jaded, let be; call off thoughts awhile
> Elsewhere;

prepares the reader for the equally relaxed conclusion which manages, unintentionally probably, to implicate the theological reference ("At God knows when to God knows what") in its chatty tone. The inclusion of the delightfully new-coined "betweenpie" inscapes, momentarily, the mile-long landscape of mountains and sky and touches the reader with its familiarity to the younger Hopkins who could draw inspiration and sustenance from natural scenery. Such a poem, along with 'Patience, hard thing!', moderates the doom and gloom that is assumed to characterise the 'terrible sonnets'.

4

Hopkins and the Critics

The first edition of Hopkins' poetry, with Bridges' apologetic introduction, appeared in 1918 and very slowly began to make its mark. By the time of the second edition in 1930, Hopkins was being noticed by poets of that time and many were surprised to discover that one of their own had been dead for half a century. Over the course of the next three or four decades Hopkins was gradually admitted into the canon, though praise and recommendation was often accompanied by a carping criticism that seemed unable to shake off the legacy of Bridges' reservations. T.S. Eliot, writing in 'After Strange Gods' in 1934, found fault with the poet because, firstly, he was too "purely verbal", too concerned with expressing and then re-expressing a sentiment, and secondly, as a consequence, lacking an argumentative edge or the ability to develop a line of thought. Such objections have not stood the test of time: the "purely verbal" becoming the very source of our enjoyment of the poetry, and the other criticism plainly wrong when put alongside poems like the Dublin sonnets.

The development of New Criticism in these decades might have been expected to have enthusiastically embraced the poetry of Hopkins because of the way this type of literary criticism focused intensively on the "purely verbal", dispensing with biographical or historical data in order to explore a work's emotional and intellectual tensions. The carping continued, though, as shown in Yvor Winters' comparison of a Donne sonnet and a poem of Bridges with poems of Hopkins. Winters' essay, for what it is worth, can be found in the *Twentieth Century Views* series title on Hopkins edited by Geoffrey Hartman, but the collection of essays in this volume is more useful for its inclusion of a section from *New Bearings in English Poetry* by F.R. Leavis. Written in 1960, Leavis draws attention to much of what is valuable in the poetry of Hopkins and the essay serves as an admirably clear introduction to the poet, not least because it focuses on the potency of the poems themselves, the subtlety of their images, and with a minimal use of literary jargon. At one stage, referring to the lines from 'The Leaden Echo and the Golden Echo' quoted earlier (page 6), he makes his point by quoting a best-forgotten critic who thought he could show how the lines could be improved upon:

> How to keep beauty? Is there any way?
> Is there nowhere any means to have it stay?
> Will no bow or brooch or braid,
> Brace or lace
> Latch or catch
> Or key to lock the door lend aid
> Before beauty vanishes away?

"There is no need to quote further," concludes Leavis with polite restraint. He brings his analysis of the poetry to a conclusion with two paragraphs summarising what he has set out to justify and demonstrate:

> He is now felt to be a contemporary, and his influence is likely to be great. It will not necessarily manifest itself in imitation of the more obvious of his technical peculiarities (these, plainly, may be dangerous toys); but no one can come from his work without an extended notion of the resources of English. And a technique so much concerned with inner division, friction, and psychological complexities in general has a special bearing on the problems of contemporary poetry. He is likely to prove, for our time and the future, the only influential poet of the Victorian age, and he seems to me the greatest.

The insights of Leavis were left behind in the 1970s and 1980s in a plethora of recondite scholarship, of the kind that often filled the pages of *The Hopkins Quarterly* as well as a number of critical studies that could charitably be described as esoteric. Some of this work came from theologians with a literary bent who set about the business of interpreting Hopkins in ways that were mainly of interest to fellow theologians. This school of criticism has not gone away, though in the 1980s and into the early 1990s, the heyday of what was then called post-structuralism and deconstruction, Hopkins inevitably received the attention of a new wave of literary critics. Post-structuralism was in love with the notion of the arbitrary nature of the linguistic sign and did not regard the object to which the sign referred as being relevant to the business of deconstructing language. The object, that which a use of language was referring to, was no more important to the identity of a linguistic sign than was the intention of its user because meaning was determined by the structure of language. The destabilising consequences of this, to which a breed of critics was giddily committed to revealing in the name of deconstruction, arose from the insight that this structure was purely constituted by a system of differences and oppositions. Hopkins was also aware of this system of differences at the heart of language but for him, of course, there were always positive terms that anchored and constituted meaning. When, spurred by etymological curiosity into compiling lists of words like "flick, fleck, flake", Hopkins noted the fine differential shades of meaning occasioned by changing the vowel while retaining the consonant sounds –

> "Flick" means to touch or strike lightly as with the end of a whip, finger, etc. To "fleck" is the next tone above flick, still meaning to touch or strike lightly (and leave a mark of the touch or stroke) but in a broader less slight manner. Hence substantively a "fleck" is a piece of light, colour, substance, etc. looking as though shaped or produced by such touches. "Flake" is a broad and decided fleck, a thin plate of something, the tone above it.

– but traced them back to an original source, an ur-sound, that rooted meaning in the physical world. Deconstructionists, abandoning any such notion of roots as a symptom and a delusion of a Western metaphysic that insisted on presence, became intoxicated with indeterminacy in language. Metaphor, in particular, exposed the fundamental drift in the linguistic sign that robbed words of any meaning that could be located outside the structure of differences. Instead, meaning arose from the play of differences and from the way the subject was positioned within language and Hopkins' use of language offered itself as a fruitful target for deconstruction. The critic J. Hillis Miller was renowned for his work on Victorian literature long before post-structuralism became the buzzword in American university departments of English and his 1963 book *The Disappearance of God* included a perceptive essay on Hopkins that is still worth reading. Hillis Miller became very much influenced by the new fashion for deconstruction after he moved to Yale and his 1985 book *The Linguistic Moment*, includes a discussion of Hopkins that reflects this influence.

J. Hillis Miller identifies two contrary impulses in Hopkins – an overt belief in the Word governing the flux of language and, undermining this principle, a submerged recognition of the play of words that escapes fixity by its continuous displacement. Metaphor becomes not a part of language but its heart and soul, a movement without origin and lacking teleological sense. Hopkins aspires to undo such confusions of Babel and restore a pristine unity to words, to the world and to his own self that is at risk of becoming lost in its own solitary consciousness. 'The Wreck of the Deutschland', construed as an extended meditation on this theme, cannot avoid recognising the fact that there is no grounded presence in language, only a set of endless verbal permutations. Such a conclusion could be the tip of a post-structuralist iceberg that would sink the poem in a sea of floating signifiers but Hillis Miller, to his credit, insists on the poem's personal dimension and keeps 'The Wreck of the Deutschland' in focus as a living poem.

The poem is seen as an attempt by Hopkins to salvage the wreck of his self from the danger of complete fragmentation and dispersal. The labyrinth of relations within language become for Hopkins the lynchpin that will unify difference, in the same kind of way that the differences in nature evoked in poems like 'Pied Beauty' were celebrated as diverse aspects of one spirit. In 'The Wreck of the Deutschland', all words and their sounds are rhymes of the divine Logos and the poem's attention to similarities of sound makes itself heard through alliteration, assonance, puns, neologisms, internal rhyme and other bewitching features of language. For Hillis Miller, however, the attempt is a glorious failure because ultimately there is no Word behind the multiplicities of words and their sounds. The nun on the ship rises to the challenge, "breasting the babble", but the pun cannot undo what the fallen tower of Babel represents and the linguistic uncertainty is not conquered – "The majesty! what did she mean?" – because there is no ur-word capable of enunciation, only its metaphors and more words, a realisation that reaches a culmination in stanza 22:

> And the word of it Sacrificed.
> But he scores it in scarlet himself on his own bespoken,
> Before-time-taken, dearest prizèd and priced –
> Stigma, signal, cinquefoil token
> For lettering of the lamb's fleece ...

The verse labours for a word that will contain all words of signification, a transcendent and primal word that will stand outside the play of difference, only to helplessly fall back on more words again. A similar listing of verbal signifiers is reached for in the climax of the poem when the nun, close to death, calls out in her ecstasy of salvation and the divine strives to be named: "There then! the Master,/Ipse, the only one, Christ, King, Head". For Hillis Miller there is no act of naming because there is no way to speak this theological metaphysic; there is only a tumble of metaphors, the very proliferation and excess of which acknowledges that there is no Word for the mystery of existence. The intensity of the search for the unsayable accounts for the density of metaphor in the poem. For this critic, then, the result is a tension in Hopkins between his conscious theory of language, which would allow for the numinous to be spoken, and an intuitive awareness that such an endeavour is problematic because language is based on differentiation and endless permutations of metaphors.

In a post-post-structuralist world two important and very different biographies of Hopkins were published. In retrospect, Robert Martin's *Gerard Manley Hopkins: A Very Private Life* (1991) can be seen as more modish than it first appeared to be. The overriding theme of the book, the homoerotic in Hopkins' life and poetry, is reflected in the choice of the last of the book's illustrations. It is a reproduction of Frederick Walker's painting, 'Bathers', complete with an enlargement of the middle section of the painting showing frisky young men in the nude.

Walker was an artist that Hopkins much admired but there is no evidence to show that this painting was ever seen by the poet. In a similar spirit, the biography makes too much sexual capital out of the possibility of a homoerotic element in Hopkins' acquaintance with a young man called Dolben. The reading of Hopkins as a closet homosexual skews the interpretation of the poetry so that, for example, the discernible sexual drama that is detected in 'The Wreck of the Deutschland' clouds out other readings of the poem.

Hopkins is also seen to merit a chapter in Richard Dellamora's *Masculine Desire – The Sexual Politics of Victorian Aestheticism* (University of North Carolina, 1990) but only two poems are looked at in any detail and the analysis is not especially enlightening. 'Felix Randal', not surprisingly, is read by the critic as an expression of sublimated homoeroticism and the landscape of 'God's Grandeur' is seen to be imbued with a divine, masculine power that connotes "unexpended seminal fluid", while the last four lines of the octet ("Generations have trod, have trod …") "suggest phobic reaction against both intercourse and male masturbation". Such views are asserted rather than argued for and many readers will feel dissatisfied with such an approach. The degree to which Hopkins repressed homosexual feelings, the nature of the pathology this gave rise to and the relationship of all this to his poetry is difficult to assess and in some respects, without seeking to deny a sexual dimension to the poetry, this kind of approach to Hopkins may seem ultimately fairly fruitless and unnecessary. Perhaps it is enough to acknowledge that Hopkins had unresolved sexual feelings, that this fact played a part in his decision to become a Jesuit and lead the kind of life he chose for himself, and that some of his poetry reflects this. There is more to the life of Hopkins than just his sexuality, or his lack thereof, and why anyway should we want to put him on the psychiatrist's couch and adopt a psychosexual approach?

Seamus Heaney delivered a lecture on Hopkins in 1974, available in his *Preoccupations: Selected prose 1968-1978* (Faber, London, 1980), that sets out an alternative understanding of the idea of the masculine in Hopkins' verse. He begins by comparing the rich symbolism of the image in Blake's 'The Sick Rose' with the use of allegory in Hopkins' 'Heaven-Haven', a very early poem, in order to show how Hopkins is not mining the symbolic power of a symbol in the way that Blake does. He then introduces a line from the poet Keats to illustrate how "Keats woos us to receive, Hopkins alerts us to perceive". These two comparisons, with Blake and Keats, are used to demonstrate how Hopkins is writing a kind of poetry that insists on being intellectual and disciplined rather than expressing or luxuriating in a state of feeling. Heaney is not expressing a value judgement, just observing how poets can go about their work in different ways. He describes Hopkins' approach: "It is the way words strike off one another, the way they are drilled, marched and countermarched, rather than the way they philander and linger among themselves, that constitutes his proper music." The point of the military versus the amorous imagery here is developed by Heaney into an opposition of Hopkins' 'masculine' poetic – an athletic, muscular shaping of words and meaning into a form of address – as opposed to a 'feminine' one of evocation and revelation, using words "drowsy from their slumber in the unconscious". A good example of what is meant here by the 'feminine' is identified by Heaney in these lines from, 'A Vision of the Mermaids', written by Hopkins as a teenager (Hopkins would later criticise this kind of poetry when he bemoaned Keats' verse for "abandoning itself to an unmanly and enervating luxury"):

> A tinted fin on either shoulder hung;
> Their pansy-dark or bronzen locks were strung
> With coral, shells, thick-pearlèd cords, whate'er
> The abysmal Ocean hoards of strange and rare.

To show how far Hopkins travelled from this kind of poetry, he looks at the fourth stanza of 'The Wreck of the Deutschland' to reveal the diagrammatic, intellectual nature of the verse:

> I am soft sift
> In an hourglass – at the wall
> Fast, but mined with a motion, a drift,
> And it crowds and it combs to the fall;
> I steady as a water in a well, to a poise, to a pane,
> But roped with, always, all the way down from the tall
> Fells or flanks of the voel, a vein
> Of the gospel proffer, a pressure, a principle, Christ's gift.

The sand in the hourglass and the water in the hills serve as analogies for what is seeming to be a sinking to the bottom (the streaming down of the sand and the downpouring of rain on the fells) but is actually a rising upwards, a spring and a source. Similarly, by way of extending the analogy, Christ's power seems dark, forbidding and terrible (as in the poem's first stanza) but is really merciful, loving and liberating (as expressed in the image of the sloe in stanza eight). This leads to stanza nine and the paradox of finding freedom in submission. In these few stanzas, Heaney traces the whole argument of the poem – "the utterance of Hopkins' whole reality, of his myth" – driven by Hopkins' need to make meaning of his life and his sense of a divine intervention in his existence.

Heaney also compares the fire imagery of stanza 10 with a similar image in 'To R.B.' to advance the idea that Hopkins sees his art and his vocation as the fertilisation of his 'feminine' powers by the disciplining will of the male divine. This, says Heaney, gave Hopkins the conviction that he could and should express in poetry, as he does in the sestet of 'The Windhover', his sense of the divine in the sensuous beauty of the world. Hopkins' God, then, is the masculine, design-making master that rules over the world's fecund beauty and, similarly, the poetic act for Hopkins becomes "a love act" that complies with the will of God while celebrating an emotional physicality. Heaney's analysis of Hopkins certainly seems to hint at some kind of psychosexual understanding of the poet's mixing of the theological with the mimetic, of religious rhetoric with rapturous pagan delight – the celibate Hopkins fertilising his feminine powers with the male will, God as "Father and fondler" – but the emphasis throughout the essay is on particulars of the verse and the reader is not encouraged to stray into murky psychoanalytic interpretations. For Heaney himself it is the voice of Hopkins, his "alliterating music" and "ricocheting con-sonants" as he puts it, that gave him the desire to write poetry himself.

The year after Heaney's lecture, 1975, saw the publication of Edward Said's *Beginnings*. Said is concerned with the nature of the writer's task and the ways in which modern writers conceive of their work in terms of a beginning rather than an origin. Instead of thinking of their writing in a dynastic way, bound to and linked with sources, the writers of literary modernism that interest Said understand their work as the act of an intentional beginning, a construction in a relationship of adjacency with what has gone before. For Said, writers like Hopkins are makers of text and single-mindedly concerned with the difficulty of this task. Writing becomes extremely problematic for modern writers like Hopkins, Joyce, Proust, Conrad and others. *Beginnings* is not an easy book for readers lacking an acquaintance with the writers under discussion and it cannot be dipped into in order to extract nuggets of 'meaning' about a particular text. What Said manages to do, however, is render as fairly simplistic the psychosexual, biographical readings of Hopkins. He offers, instead, a more complex and a more richly contextualised account of the way the poet saw his work as analogous to God's creation of being. The felt loss of creativity on Hopkins' becomes entangled with his deep perplexity over his artistic desires and images of sterility haunt his later years and the Dublin sonnets.

To return briefly to biographies, Norman White's scholarly *Hopkins: A Literary Biography*, is a far more judicious account of the poet's life. As well as detailing the course of a remarkably uneventful and unglamorous life, White offers short but pertinent comments on the poetry of his subject. The biography brings out the winsome character of the poet without being uncritical and, best of all, it is likely to encourage the reader to read the poems and enjoy them.

Norman White's *Hopkins in Ireland* was published in 2002, ten years after the biography, and it focuses on the final years of the poet's life. It is a masterly study of Hopkins' pained state of mind and the poems he wrote in Ireland, refreshingly free of theological waffle. The final poems are explored in detail and there is an excellent line-by-line analysis of 'Spelt from Sibyl's Leaves'.

Conclusion

In the end it is Hopkins' openness to the resilience of Being and
its sensuous physicality, the Heidegger-like experience of being-
in-the-world and the inscape of self, the close attention to
relationships of texture, colour and motion in things, seasonal
change and the patterns in nature, the celebration of innocence
and the pain of experience, the moral audacity – these are the
keys to his strength as a poet. His linguistic virtuosity summons
up the elemental energies of words in order to reach something
essential about our response to being in the world. Hopkins'
mining and miming of language and the unforced chiselling-
out of meaning is not didactic in any sense, despite the
theological intent, because he is not drawing out a moral or
impressing an ethic. Like Heidegger, a philosopher who also
returned to Pre-Socratic thinkers like Parmenides for inspiration
(and whose doctoral dissertation was on Duns Scotus), Hopkins
raises and foregrounds ontological issues. The poetry seeks the
revelation of Being through an act of imaginative apprehension,
hence the physicality, corporeality and tactility that the language
is called upon to express, whether speaking of God's power
("Over again I feel thy finger and find thee"), a ploughman ("the
rack of ribs; the scooped flank; lank/Rope-over thigh") or the
mind itself (with its "mountains; cliffs of fall/Frightful, sheer,
no-man-fathomed"). Hopkins wants us to respond to Being and,
just as it became the focus of thinking for the later Heidegger,
the nature of poetry and language becomes central to this act of
responding. We are reminded that poetry is capable of a unique
sensitivity to the richness of meaning and Hopkins draws on

the power of language in order to reveal Being anew.

Any rounded assessment of Hopkins as a poet needs to acknowledge that sometimes his drawing on the power of language leads him or the reader at least, to poems that work too hard and run the risk of failing to communicate. There is nothing wrong with having to consult explanatory notes in order to be clear about a particular word or image but there are times when, after such consultation, lines of a poem still fail to engage the reader.

There is another quality, another dimension, to Hopkins and his poetry that is crucial to his importance and to our appreciation of his work. Like the existentialist philosophers, existence becomes an issue for Hopkins. It is not enough to be in the world, there are choices to be made and commitments to be contemplated if one is to exist resolutely. There is a danger of our being dispersing into different worldly activities – the blearing and smearing of 'God's Grandeur' – and we need to gather ourselves up and work against the dispersion. What becomes important is our attitude towards life, and towards our death, and the way we conduct our being so as to seize on existence and confront it authentically. In his younger years, when his life seemed so full of promise, Hopkins gave expression to his authenticity in those marvelous poems he composed in Wales. They were inseparable from the way he chose to live his life – "What I do is me: for that I came" – they were his praxis. Echoing the claims of Aristotle and Hegel, and most especially Marx, that the self is what it does, Hopkins knew that his life's activities would be the concrete embodiment of who he was. Choosing to be a priest, a Jesuit priest in particular, was a demonstration of Hopkins' authenticity.

Marx realised and explained the consequences that follow, in our world, from the fact that the very nature and character of a person is determined by what he does. In an alienated world, man becomes estranged not only from the products he shapes in his work but also from the very process and activity of that work, so that people become alienated from each other and from themselves. This is what gradually happened to Hopkins, crystallizing after his move to Ireland, and his vulnerability as a person made the experience particularly painful. His work as a priest became less and less satisfying; hence his heartfelt complaints about the drudgery of marking examination scripts in Dublin, and the almost unbearable self-alienation of his last sonnets.

On one occasion as a young man, Hopkins admitted in his journal to feeling downcast and the effect was for him to lose his sense of the wholeness of the natural world: "nature in all her parcels and faculties gaped and fell apart, like a clod cleaving and holding only by strings of root. But this must often be." Hopkins' life, like many lives, was akin to this in some ways: seeking coherence and meaning and enjoying moments of rapture but at other times feeling fragile and fractured, susceptible to melancholy and awful loneliness yet hanging on in the absence of any viable alternative. It was out of these real-life struggles and tensions that the writing came, hence the voice of authenticity in the poetry; a voice that delivered a self-verdict not far from the mark: "Some of my rhymes I regret, but they are past changing, grubs in amber: there are only a few of these; others are unassailable; some others again there are which malignity may munch at but the Muses love."

It seems right that Hopkins should call upon the Muses, the nine daughters of Zeus and Mnemosyne who inspired Homer, to justify his verse because, ultimately, it is the voice of a pagan religiosity that speaks to us in his poetry. It also becomes the voice of a lonely and rare individual who casts light, momentarily, before fading away, leaving behind his poetry:

> Sometimes a lantern moves along the night.
> That interests our eyes. And who goes there?
> I think; where from and bound, I wonder, where,
> With, all down darkness wide, his wading light?

Men go by me whom either beauty bright
In mould or mind or what not else makes rare:
They rain against our much-thick and marsh air
Rich beams, till death or distance buys them quite.

Further reading

Poetry and prose
Gerard Manley Hopkins: Poetry and Prose, edited by Walford Davies (J.M. Dent, Orion Publishing, 2002). A very useful edition of the poetry, with selected prose extracts from Hopkins' diaries and journals, letters and devotional writings, as well as extracts from modern literary critics and helpful explanatory notes to the poems.
The Poems of Gerard Manley Hopkins, 4th edition, edited by W.H. Gardner and N.H. MacKenzie, (Oxford University Press, 1970). A scholarly edition, brings together all the known poems and fragments.

Biographies
Hopkins: A Literary Biography, Norman White (Oxford University Press, 1992)
Gerard Manley Hopkins: A Very Private Life, Robert Bernard Martin (HarperCollins, 1991).

Criticism
A Collection of Critical Essays, 'Twentieth-Century Views' series, edited by Geoffrey H. Hartman (Prentice-Hall, 1966). Now out of print but worth seeking out in a library for its inclusion of essays by F.R. Leavis, J. Hillis Miller and Geoffrey H. Hartman.
A Reader's Guide to Gerard Manley Hopkins, N.H. MacKenzie (Thames and Hudson, 1981).

'The Fire I'the Flint: Reflections on the Poetry of Gerard Manley Hopkins', in *Preoccupations*, Seamus Heaney (Faber, 1981).

The Linguistic Moment: From Wordsworth to Stevens, J. Hillis Miller (Princeton University Press, 1985).

Hopkins in Ireland, Norman White (University College Dublin Press, 2002)

The Disappearance of God: Five Nineteenth-Century Writers, J. Hillis Miller (Harvard University Press, 1963). The section on Hopkins, 'The Univocal Chiming', is reprinted in Hartman's *A Collection of Critical Essays*.

Gerard Manley Hopkins, edited by Harold Bloom (Chelsea House Publishing, 1986). Includes Hartman's essay, 'The Dialectic of Sense-Perception', reprinted in Hartman's *A Collection of Critical Essays*.

A Preface to Hopkins, 'Preface Books' series, Graham Storey (Longman, 1981).

Rereading Hopkins: Selected New Essays, edited by Francis L. Fennell (University of Victoria, 1996).

'Hopkins: Agonistic Reactionary', in *Victorian Poetry*, Isobel Armstrong (Routledge, 1993).

Hopkins' Idealism: Philosophy, Physics, Poetry, Daniel Brown (Oxford University Press, 2001).

'Helmholtz, Tyndall, Gerard Manley Hopkins: Leaps of the Prepared Imagination' in *Open Fields: Science in Cultural Encounter*, Gillian Beer (Clarendon Press, 1999)

Beginnings, Edward Said (Granta, 1997).

Website

www.gerardmanleyhopkins.org/festival (Gerard Manley Hopkins International Summer School)

GREENWICH EXCHANGE BOOKS

STUDENT GUIDE LITERARY SERIES

The Greenwich Exchange Student Guide Literary Series is a collection of critical essays of major or contemporary serious writers in English and selected European languages. The series is for the student, the teacher and 'common readers' and is an ideal resource for libraries. The *Times Educational Supplement* praised these books, saying, "The style of [this series] has a pressure of meaning behind it. Readers should learn from that ... If art is about selection, perception and taste, then this is it."

(ISBN prefix 1-871551- applies)
All books are paperbacks unless otherwise stated

The series includes:
W.H. Auden by Stephen Wade (36-6)
Honoré de Balzac by Wendy Mercer (48-X)
William Blake by Peter Davies (27-7)
The Brontës by Peter Davies (24-2)
Robert Browning by John Lucas (59-5)
Byron by Andrew Keanie (83-9)
Samuel Taylor Coleridge by Andrew Keanie (64-1)
Joseph Conrad by Martin Seymour-Smith (18-8)
William Cowper by Michael Thorn (25-0)
Charles Dickens by Robert Giddings (26-9)
Emily Dickinson by Marnie Pomeroy (68-4)
John Donne by Seán Haldane (23-4)
Ford Madox Ford by Anthony Fowles (63-3)
The Stagecraft of Brian Friel by David Grant (74-9)
Robert Frost by Warren Hope (70-6)
Thomas Hardy by Sean Haldane (33-1)
Seamus Heaney by Warren Hope (37-4)
Joseph Heller by Anthony Fowles (84-6)
Gerard Manley Hopkins by Sean Sheehan (77-3)
James Joyce by Michael Murphy (73-0)
Philip Larkin by Warren Hope (35-8)
Laughter in the Dark – The Plays of Joe Orton by Arthur Burke (56-0)
Poets of the First World War by John Greening (79-X)
Philip Roth by Paul McDonald (72-2)
Shakespeare's *Macbeth* by Matt Simpson (69-2)

Shakespeare's *Othello* by Matt Simpson (71-4)
Shakespeare's *The Tempest* by Matt Simpson (75-7)
Shakespeare's *Twelfth Night* by Matt Simpson (86-2)
Shakespeare's **Non-Dramatic Poetry** by Martin Seymour-Smith (22-6)
Shakespeare's **Sonnets** by Martin Seymour-Smith (38-2)
Shakespeare's *The Winter's Tale* by John Lucas (80-3)
Tobias Smollett by Robert Giddings (21-8)
Dylan Thomas by Peter Davies (78-1)
Alfred, Lord Tennyson by Michael Thorn (20-X)
William Wordsworth by Andrew Keanie (57-9)
W.B. Yeats by John Greening (34-X)

LITERATURE & BIOGRAPHY

Matthew Arnold and 'Thyrsis' *by Patrick Carill Connolly*
Matthew Arnold (1822-1888) was a leading poet, intellect and aesthete of the Victorian epoch. He is now best known for his strictures as a literary and cultural critic, and educationist. After a long period of neglect, his views have come in for a re-evaluation. Arnold's poetry remains less well known, yet his poems and his understanding of poetry, which defied the conventions of his time, were central to his achievement.

The author traces Arnold's intellectual and poetic development, showing how his poetry gathers its meanings from a lifetime's study of European literature and philosophy. Connolly's unique exegesis of 'Thyrsis' draws upon a wide-ranging analysis of the pastoral and its associated myths in both classical and native cultures. This study shows lucidly and in detail how Arnold encouraged the intense reflection of the mind on the subject placed before it, believing in " ... the all importance of the choice of the subject, the necessity of accurate observation; and subordinate character of expression."

Patrick Carill Connolly gained his English degree at Reading University and taught English literature abroad for a number of years before returning to Britain. He is now a civil servant living in London.
2004 • 180 pages • ISBN 1-871551-61-7

The Author, the Book and the Reader *by Robert Giddings*
This collection of essays analyses the effects of changing technology and the attendant commercial pressures on literary styles and subject matter. Authors covered include Charles Dickens, Tobias Smollett, Mark Twain, Dr Johnson and John le Carré.
1991 • 220 pages • illustrated • ISBN 1-871551-01-3

Aleister Crowley and the Cult of Pan *by Paul Newman*

Few more nightmarish figures stalk English literature than Aleister Crowley (1875-1947), poet, magician, mountaineer and agent provocateur. In this groundbreaking study, Paul Newman dives into the occult mire of Crowley's works and fishes out gems and grotesqueries that are by turns ethereal, sublime, pornographic and horrifying. Like Oscar Wilde before him, Crowley stood in "symbolic relationship to his age" and to contemporaries like Rupert Brooke, G.K. Chesterton and the Portuguese modernist, Fernando Pessoa. An influential exponent of the cult of the Great God Pan, his essentially 'pagan' outlook was shared by major European writers as well as English novelists like E.M. Forster, D.H. Lawrence and Arthur Machen.

Paul Newman lives in Cornwall. Editor of the literary magazine *Abraxas*, he has written more than ten books.

2004 • 222 pages • ISBN 1-871551-66-8

John Dryden *by Anthony Fowles*

Of all the poets of the Augustan age, John Dryden was the most worldly. Anthony Fowles traces Dryden's evolution from 'wordsmith' to major poet. This critical study shows a poet of vigour and technical panache whose art was forged in the heat and battle of a turbulent polemical and pamphleteering age. Although Dryden's status as a literary critic has long been established, Fowles draws attention to his neglected achievements as a translator of poetry. He deals also with the less well-known aspects of Dryden's work – his plays and occasional pieces.

Born in London and educated at the Universities of Oxford and Southern California, Anthony Fowles began his career in film-making before becoming an author of film and television scripts and more than twenty books. Readers will welcome the many contemporary references to novels and film with which Fowles illuminates the life and work of this decisively influential English poetic voice.

2003 • 292 pages • ISBN 1-871551-58-7

The Good That We Do *by John Lucas*

John Lucas' book blends fiction, biography and social history in order to tell the story of his grandfather, Horace Kelly. Headteacher of a succession of elementary schools in impoverished areas of London, 'Hod' Kelly was also a keen cricketer, a devotee of the music hall, and included among his friends the great trade union leader, Ernest Bevin. In telling the story of his life, Lucas has provided a fascinating range of insights into the lives of ordinary Londoners from the First World War until the outbreak of the Second World War. Threaded throughout is an account of such people's hunger for education, and of the different ways government, church and educational officialdom ministered to that hunger. *The Good That We Do* is both a study of one man and of a period when England changed, drastically and forever.

John Lucas is Professor Emeritus of the Universities of Loughborough and Nottingham Trent. He is the author of numerous works of a critical and scholarly nature and has published seven collections of poetry.

2001 • 214 pages • ISBN 1-871551-54-4

In Pursuit of Lewis Carroll *by Raphael Shaberman*

Sherlock Holmes and the author uncover new evidence in their investigations into the mysterious life and writing of Lewis Carroll. They examine published works by Carroll that have been overlooked by previous commentators. A newly-discovered poem, almost certainly by Carroll, is published here.

Amongst many aspects of Carroll's highly complex personality, this book explores his relationship with his parents, numerous child friends, and the formidable Mrs Liddell, mother of the immortal Alice. Raphael Shaberman was a founder member of the Lewis Carroll Society and a teacher of autistic children.

1994 • 118 pages • illustrated • ISBN 1-871551-13-7

Liar! Liar!: Jack Kerouac – Novelist *by R.J. Ellis*

The fullest study of Jack Kerouac's fiction to date. It is the first book to devote an individual chapter to every one of his novels. *On the Road*, *Visions of Cody* and *The Subterraneans* are reread in-depth, in a new and exciting way. *Visions of Gerard* and *Doctor Sax* are also strikingly reinterpreted, as are other daringly innovative writings, like 'The Railroad Earth' and his "try at a spontaneous *Finnegans Wake*" – *Old Angel Midnight*. Neglected writings, such as *Tristessa* and *Big Sur*, are also analysed, alongside better-known novels such as *Dharma Bums* and *Desolation Angels*.

R.J. Ellis is Senior Lecturer in English at Nottingham Trent University.

1999 • 294 pages • ISBN 1-871551-53-6

Musical Offering *by Yolanthe Leigh*

In a series of vivid sketches, anecdotes and reflections, Yolanthe Leigh tells the story of her growing up in the Poland of the 1930s and the Second World War. These are poignant episodes of a child's first encounters with both the enchantments and the cruelties of the world; and from a later time, stark memories of the brutality of the Nazi invasion, and the hardships of student life in Warsaw under the Occupation. But most of all this is a record of inward development; passages of remarkable intensity and simplicity describe the girl's response to religion, to music, and to her discovery of philosophy.

Yolanthe Leigh was formerly a Lecturer in Philosophy at Reading University.

2000 • 56 pages • ISBN: 1-871551-46-3

Norman Cameron *by Warren Hope*
Norman Cameron's poetry was admired by W.H. Auden, celebrated by Dylan Thomas and valued by Robert Graves. He was described by Martin Seymour-Smith as, "one of ... the most rewarding and pure poets of his generation ..." and is at last given a full-length biography. This eminently sociable man, who had periods of darkness and despair, wrote little poetry by comparison with others of his time, but it is always of a consistently high quality – imaginative and profound.

2000 • 220 pages • illustrated • ISBN 1-871551-05-6

POETRY

Adam's Thoughts in Winter *by Warren Hope*
Warren Hope's poems have appeared from time to time in a number of literary periodicals, pamphlets and anthologies on both sides of the Atlantic. They appeal to lovers of poetry everywhere. His poems are brief, clear, frequently lyrical, characterised by wit, but often distinguished by tenderness. The poems gathered in this first book-length collection counter the brutalising ethos of contemporary life, speaking of, and for, the virtues of modesty, honesty and gentleness in an individual, memorable way.

2000 • 46 pages • ISBN 1-871551-40-4

Baudelaire: Les Fleurs du Mal *Translated by F.W. Leakey*
Selected poems from *Les Fleurs du Mal* are translated with parallel French texts and are designed to be read with pleasure by readers who have no French as well as those who are practised in the French language.

F.W. Leakey was Professor of French in the University of London. As a scholar, critic and teacher he specialised in the work of Baudelaire for 50 years and published a number of books on the poet.

2001 • 152 pages • ISBN 1-871551-10-2

'The Last Blackbird' and other poems by Ralph Hodgson *edited and introduced by John Harding*
Ralph Hodgson (1871-1962) was a poet and illustrator whose most influential and enduring work appeared to great acclaim just prior to, and during, the First World War. His work is imbued with a spiritual passion for

the beauty of creation and the mystery of existence. This new selection brings together, for the first time in 40 years, some of the most beautiful and powerful 'hymns to life' in the English language.

John Harding lives in London. He is a freelance writer and teacher and is Ralph Hodgson's biographer.

2004 • 70 pages • ISBN 1-871551-81-1

Lines from the Stone Age *by Sean Haldane*
Reviewing Sean Haldane's 1992 volume *Desire in Belfast*, Robert Nye wrote in *The Times* that "Haldane can be sure of his place among the English poets." This place is not yet a conspicuous one, mainly because his early volumes appeared in Canada, and because he has earned his living by other means than literature. Despite this, his poems have always had their circle of readers. The 60 previously unpublished poems of *Lines from the Stone Age* – "lines of longing, terror, pride, lust and pain" – may widen this circle.

2000 • 52 pages • ISBN 1-871551-39-0

Shakespeare's Sonnets *by Martin Seymour-Smith*
Martin Seymour-Smith's outstanding achievement lies in the field of literary biography and criticism. In 1963 he produced his comprehensive edition, in the old spelling, of *Shakespeare's Sonnets* (here revised and corrected by himself and Peter Davies in 1998). With its landmark introduction and its brilliant critical commentary on each sonnet, it was praised by William Empson and John Dover Wilson. Stephen Spender said of him "I greatly admire Martin Seymour-Smith for the independence of his views and the great interest of his mind"; and both Robert Graves and Anthony Burgess described him as the leading critic of his time. His exegesis of the *Sonnets* remains unsurpassed.

2001 • 194 pages • ISBN 1-871551-38-2

The Rain and the Glass *by Robert Nye*
When Robert Nye's first poems were published, G.S. Fraser declared in the *Times Literary Supplement*: "Here is a proper poet, though it is hard to see how the larger literary public (greedy for flattery of their own concerns) could be brought to recognize that. But other proper poets – how many of them are left? – will recognize one of themselves."

Since then Nye has become known to a large public for his novels, especially *Falstaff* (1976), winner of the Hawthornden Prize and The Guardian Fiction Prize, and *The Late Mr Shakespeare* (1998). But his true vocation has always been poetry, and it is as a poet that he is best known to his fellow poets. "Nye is the inheritor of a poetic tradition that runs from Donne and Ralegh to Edward Thomas and Robert Graves," wrote James Aitchison in 1990, while the critic Gabriel Josipovici has described him as "one of the most interesting poets writing today, with a voice unlike that of any of his contemporaries".

This book contains all the poems Nye has written since his *Collected Poems* of 1995, together with his own selection from that volume. An introduction, telling the story of his poetic beginnings, affirms Nye's unfashionable belief in inspiration, as well as defining that quality of unforced truth which distinguishes the best of his work: "I have spent my life trying to write poems, but the poems gathered here came mostly when I was not."

2005 • 132 pages • ISBN 1-871551-41-2

Wilderness *by Martin Seymour-Smith*
This is Martin Seymour-Smith's first publication of his poetry for more than twenty years. This collection of 36 poems is a fearless account of an inner life of love, frustration, guilt, laughter and the celebration of others. He is best known to the general public as the author of the controversial and bestselling *Hardy* (1994).

1994 • 52 pages • ISBN 1-871551-08-0

BUSINESS

English Language Skills *by Vera Hughes*
If you want to be sure, (as a student, or in your business or personal life), that your written English is correct, this book is for you. Vera Hughes' aim is to help you to remember the basic rules of spelling, grammar and punctuation. 'Noun', 'verb', 'subject', 'object' and 'adjective' are the only technical terms used. The book teaches the clear, accurate English required by the business and office world. It coaches acceptable current usage and makes the rules easier to remember.

Vera Hughes was a civil servant and is a trainer and author of training manuals.

2002 • 142 pages • ISBN 1-871551-60-9